Dearest M

Wishing you a Very happy Birthday --

a Wee Pressie —

Rather fitting As its the year of the Olympics in England, + My lovely Evening spent with you + Soph — for the Opening Ceremony xx

Lots of Love x

x [signature] x

x xx

The
Olympic Games
Miscellany

First published in 2008
This edition published in 2011

Copyright © Carlton Books Limited 2008, 2011

London 2012 emblem(s) © The London Organising Committee of
the Olympic Games and Paralympic Games Ltd (LOCOG) 2007.
London 2012 Pictograms © LOCOG 2009. All rights reserved.

Carlton Books Limited
20 Mortimer Street
London W1T 3JW

A CIP catalogue record for this book is available
from the British Library

ISBN: 978-1-84732-843-4

Editor: Martin Corteel
Project Direction Darren Jordan
Production: Janette Burgin

Printed in Great Britain

The Olympic Games Miscellany

John White

with a foreword by Dame Mary Peters, DBE

An official London 2012 Olympic Games publication

CARLTON

Foreword

I was delighted when John approached me to write the foreword to his book. As a youngster growing up in Liverpool I enjoyed an outdoor life. I was a bit of a tomboy and, looking back, I suppose the Olympic Games ideology was in me from an early age. In 1950, my father's business meant we had to move to Northern Ireland to live, and while a pupil at Ballymena Intermediate School I won my first trophy, a shield for the best all-round athlete. When we moved to Armagh a few years later my headmaster at Portadown College recognised that I had a certain degree of athletic potential and introduced me to the school's athletics coach, Kenneth McClelland. Ken coached me in the sprints, high jump and long jump and encouraged me to participate in the inaugural Northern Ireland pentathlon competition. I finished third behind Thelma Hopkins and Maeve Kyle, both Olympians.

I took part in my first Olympic Games in Tokyo in 1964, finishing fourth in the women's Pentathlon. I managed a silver medal in the shot put at the 1966 Commonwealth Games and was very honoured to be named the Ladies GB Team Captain for Mexico City 1968. I had a disappointing time, finishing ninth in the women's Pentathlon. However, at the 1970 Commonwealth Games, I managed a double gold, winning the pentathlon and the shot put. And so on to Munich 1972 … My own memories from Munich are beating the home favourite, Heidi Rosendahl, albeit by just ten points, and achieving four personal bests on my way to setting a new world record score of 4,801 points for the event. Two years later, I retained my Commonwealth Games gold medal.

Although Munich was my final Olympic Games as a competitor, my experiences of the event were far from over. I worked for BBC Radio at Montreal 1976 and was the GB Ladies Team Manager for Moscow 1980 and Los Angeles 1984. In 1988, I covered the Seoul Games for New Zealand Radio, and I attended the following four Games as a voluntary representative of the British Olympic Association. Sport has been my life and I have had the privilege of meeting many wonderful people. My success in Munich helped me raise the monies to build the Mary Peters Track and set up the Ulster Sports Trust, which assists up-and-coming young Northern Ireland athletes. Who knows, we may even see one of these young people standing on a podium at the London 2012 Games.

Dame Mary Peters, DBE

Introduction

We all have our own abiding memories of the 'greatest show on earth', while past Olympic Games have provided the world with some truly remarkable achievements and many moments of nail-biting tension. My own memories from previous Games go back to 1972 and Mary Peters winning the gold medal in the women's Pentathlon. We called her 'Our Golden Girl' because, although she was born in Liverpool, Mary spent most of her life in Northern Ireland where I was born. And I was extremely proud and honoured when Dame Mary Peters, sorry Mary P, agreed to write the foreword to my book. Thanks, Our Mary!

So I hope that reading this book brings back many wonderful sporting memories for you, whether it is Jesse Owens and his sweep of four gold medals at the 1936 Games in Berlin; Ann Packer's gold medal in the women's 800m at the 1964 Olympic Games in Tokyo; David Hemery's gold medal success in the men's 400m Hurdles at Mexico City 1968; and Mark Spitz's haul of seven gold medals at Munich 1972. Or maybe your fond recollections are of Olga Korbut and Nadia Comaneci gliding effortlessly across our television screens at Montreal in 1976, with Nadia scoring the first ever perfect ten; the Coe-Ovett head-to-heads at Moscow 1980; the magnificent performances of Carl Lewis at Los Angeles 1984; the smiles of Steve Redgrave and Sally Gunnell after winning gold at Barcelona 1992; or Kelly Holmes's double gold medal win at Athens 2004, in the city where the Games began in 776 BC. Whatever your own memory, enjoy.

John White

Athens 1896

On 6 April 1896, His Majesty King George I officially opened the inaugural modern Olympic Games. Fittingly, Athens 1896 played host to the Games of the I Olympiad. A total of 241 athletes (all male) from 14 different countries participated in 43 events across nine sports. France, Great Britain, Germany and the host nation, Greece, had the highest number of delegates. Winners were presented with a silver medal and an olive branch. The Closing Ceremony took place on 15 April 1896.

Final medals table (top ten)

Pos.	Nation	Gold	Silver	Bronze	Total
1	United States	11	7	2	20
2	Greece	10	17	19	46
3	Germany	6	5	2	13
4	France	5	4	2	11
5	Great Britain	2	3	2	7
6	Hungary	2	1	3	6
7	Austria	2	1	2	5
8	Australia	2	0	0	2
9	Denmark	1	2	3	6
10	Switzerland	1	2	0	3

The flying Dane

At the 1960 Games in Rome, Denmark's Paul Elvstrom won a fourth consecutive gold medal in Sailing. At London 1948 he won the Freefly class and then in Helsinki 1952, Melbourne 1956 and Rome 1960 he claimed the gold medal in the Finn class. Elvstrom revolutionised dinghy Sailing by pioneering the technique of 'hiking' (also known as 'sitting out'); he was the first to fix straps (toe-straps) in the bottom of his dinghy. He also invented the 'kicking strap', a device to help the boat go faster by keeping the sail flatter and allowing it to maximise the wind. It left his rivals puzzled over how he managed to reach such high speeds. However, before he came ashore he removed all evidence of the straps, knowing only too well that his competitors would copy his invention.

Oak trees for the winners

In addition to a medal, the winning athletes at Berlin 1936 were presented with a winner's crown and an oak tree in a pot.

A late entry

At the 1996 Games in Atlanta, Hungarian tennis player Virag Csurgo was entered into the women's Doubles event. On the morning of 24 July, she was warming up with a team-mate when a Hungarian team official told her that one of the Singles entrants had failed to show up and that Csurgo could replace her in that tournament if she could reach the court in time for the first-round match – beginning in five minutes. Csurgo ran to the venue, still wearing her practice T-shirt and shorts, and beat her Polish opponent, Aleksandra Olsza, 6–2, 7–5. However, she lost her second-round match 6–2, 6–3 to the number eight seed from Japan, Kimiko Date. The Final was won by Lindsay Davenport of the USA, who defeated Arantxa Sanchez-Vicario from Spain 7–6, 6–2.

Disappointing medal haul

Great Britain won a total of 15 medals at the Atlanta 1996 Games; one gold (rowers Steve Redgrave and Matthew Pinsent in the Coxless pairs), eight silver and six bronze medals in comparison to the 20 medals the team had won four years earlier in Barcelona (five gold, three silver and 12 bronze). Those to win silver medals at Atlanta 1996 were Jonathan Edwards (Triple Jump), Ben Ainslie (Sailing, Open Laser Class), Steve Backley (Javelin), Roger Black (Athletics, 400m), Paul Palmer (Swimming, 400m Freestyle), Jamie Baulch, Roger Black, Marc Richardson and Mark Hylton (Athletics, 4 x 400m Relay), John Merricks and Ian Walker (Sailing, 470 Class) and Neil Broad and Tim Henman (Tennis, Doubles).

Hand-in-hand

At the 1992 Games in Barcelona, Derartu Tulu from Ethiopia won the women's 10,000m Final to become the Games' first female black African champion. In the final lap she took the lead and went on to win with Elana Meyer, a white South African, finishing second and Lynn Jennings (USA) third. When Meyer crossed the finish line, Tulu took her opponent's hand and the two athletes set off on a victory lap, symbolising a fresh start for a new Africa.

Land of the Rising Sun

The 1912 Olympic Games in Stockholm were the first with the participation of athletes from Japan.

Olympic Games talk (1)

'When I came back to my native country, after all the stories about Hitler, I couldn't ride in the front of the bus. I had to go to the back door. I couldn't live where I wanted. I wasn't invited to shake hands with Hitler, but I wasn't invited to the White House to shake hands with the President, either."

Jesse Owens, *winner of four gold medals at the 1936 Games in Berlin, following reports that Hitler refused to shake his hand*

Olympia revisited

At Athens 2004, Kristin Heaston of the USA became the first woman to compete at the ancient site of Olympia when she took the first throw in the opening event, the women's Shot Put. However, it was Cuba's Yumileidi Cumba who became the first woman to win a gold medal at Olympia with a throw of 19.59 metres.

Soviet Union's brightest star

Gymnast Larysa Latynina of the Soviet Union is the only athlete in any sport to have won 18 medals in her career at the Olympic Games. Her tally comprises nine gold, five silver and four bronze medals. In addition, she is one of only five athletes in the Games' history to have won nine gold medals and is the only athlete to have won 14 medals in individual events. Latynina is also one of only three women to have won the same event three times (the Floor Competition in 1956, 1960 and 1964). Her impressive medal haul reads: women's Artistic Team gold (1956), women's All-Around gold (1956), women's Vault gold (1956), women's Floor gold (1956), women's Uneven Bars silver (1956), Team Portable Apparatus bronze (1956), women's Team gold (1960), women's All-Around gold (1960), women's Floor gold (1960), women's Uneven Bars silver (1960), women's Balance Beam silver (1960), women's Vault bronze (1960), women's Team gold (1964), women's Floor gold (1964), women's All-Around silver (1964), women's Vault silver (1964), women's Uneven Bars bronze (1964) and women's Balance Beam bronze (1964).

The Olympic Relay

The Athletics events at London 1908 included, for the first time, a relay (called the Olympic Relay). The first two athletes ran 200 metres, the third ran 400m and fourth and last ran 800m.

Olympic curse for the Seoul man

On 26 May 1984, Soviet Union pole vaulter Sergei Bubka broke the world record in Bratislava with a vault of 5.85 metres and then broke it twice more, raising it to 5.88m and 5.90m, the latter being achieved in London on 13 July, just 15 days before the start of the 1984 Olympic Games in Los Angeles. However, Bubka was unable to compete at the Games because the USSR boycotted them. In Bubka's absence Pierre Quinon from France won the men's Pole Vault gold medal with a vault 12 centimetres lower than Bubka's world record. Bubka took his first and only Olympic Games medal ar Seoul 1988, winning gold with a vault of 5.90m – but only just, as it was his third and final attempt. Prior to the 1992 Olympic Games in Barcelona, Bubka had raised the world record to 6.11m in Dijon, France. However, his Olympic Games curse struck when he failed to clear the bar in his first three attempts and crashed out of the competition. Four years later, at Atlanta 1996, a heel injury forced him to withdraw from the competition without making a vault and then at the 2000 Games in Sydney, he did not register a score in the final after three failed attempts to clear 5.70m. During his outstanding career, Bubka won a magnificent array of medals, claiming six consecutive IAAF World Championship golds (1983–97) and one European Championships gold medal (Stuttgart 1986). He broke the world record 35 times in his career, 17 times outdoors and 18 times indoors, often by only one or two centimetres. 'I love the pole vault because it is a professor's sport,' Bubka once said. 'One must not only run and jump, but one must think. Which pole to use, which height to jump, which strategy to use. I love it because the results are immediate and the strongest is the winner. Everyone knows it. In everyday life that is difficult to prove.'

Intercalated Games

In 1906, Baron Pierre de Coubertin permitted Greece to stage an Intercalated Games in Athens as compensation for the country losing the right to host every Summer Games. Although the International Olympic Committee does not officially recognise the 1906 Games, despite the fact that they were organised by them, many historians consider the 1906 Intercalated Games as a proper Olympic Games.

Did you know that?
Great Britain won eight gold, 11 silver and six bronze medals at the 1906 Intercalated Games in Athens.

Men's 100m Fantasy Olympic Games Final

Lane No./Athlete	Country	Medals
1 Carl Lewis	USA	2 Golds – Los Angeles 1984 and Seoul 1988
2 Archie Hahn	USA	2 Golds – St Louis 1904 and Athens 1906*
3 Jesse Owens	USA	Gold – Berlin 1936
4 Donovan Bailey	CAN	Gold – Atlanta 1996
5 Maurice Greene	USA	Gold – Sydney 2000, Silver – Athens 2004
6 Valeri Borzov	USSR	Gold – Moscow 1980, Bronze – Montreal 1976
7 Usain Bolt	JAM	Gold – Beijing 2008
8 Harold Abrahams	GB	Gold – Paris 1924

* Intercalated Games

A popular winner

Spyridon Louis, a Greek shepherd, pleased the host nation at Athens 1896 when he raced to victory in the men's Marathon. Louis was born on 12 January 1873 in Maroussi, near Athens. Of all the events at the first modern Games the hosts wanted to win the 40,000m men's Marathon race more than any other. The endurance race was specifically created in honour of the legend of Pheidippides, a Greek hero who allegedly carried the news of the Greek victory at the Battle of Marathon in 490 BC by running from Marathon to Athens. With four kilometres left to race, Louis took the lead in a field of 17 runners and, to the delight of the 100,000 spectators located in and around the Panathenaic Stadium, he won the race by more than seven minutes. Some 40 years after his famous victory, Louis recalled the moments directly after he crossed the winning line: 'That hour was something unimaginable and it still appears to me in my memory like a dream... Twigs and flowers were raining down on me. Everybody was calling out my name and throwing their hats in the air.' Louis remained a national hero until his death on 26 March 1940. He participated in only one Olympic Games. Louis did not own any shoes and to race in the men's Marathon he wore shoes paid for by people from local villages.

Greatest ever wrestler

At Tokyo 1964, 24-year-old Japanese wrestler Osamu Watanabe, in his first Games, delighted his home nation by winning the Freestyle Wrestling gold medal in the Feather Weight division. Amazingly, Watanabe went through the competition without giving up any points (his aggregate score was 186–0) and spent only ten minutes on the mats on his way to claiming gold. He retired after the Games, making him the only modern Olympian in any style of Wrestling to go unbeaten throughout the entirety of his career and without conceding any points.

Super Eagles swoop to take gold

Each team that qualified for the men's Football tournament at Atlanta 1996 could include three professional players, regardless of their age or previous Games experience. The Super Eagles of Nigeria won the men's tournament, with Argentina claiming silver and Brazil bronze. In the women's tournament, the USA beat China in the final, while Norway defeated Brazil in the bronze-medal game.

Paris 1900

On 14 May 1900, the Games of the II Olympiad officially opened in Paris, France. The Games were held as part of the Exposition Universelle Internationale, also known as the Paris World's Fair. Four years after the staging of the inaugural modern Games women made their first appearance at the event. A total of 997 athletes (975 male and 22 female) from 24 different countries participated in 95 events across 18 sports. The organizers of the Exposition/World's Fair spread the 95 events contested over a period of five months, and the Closing Ceremony took place on 28 October. As a result, the profile of the events was so low that many athletes died without ever knowing that they had actually participated at the Olympic Games.

Final medals table (top ten)

Pos.	Nation	Gold	Silver	Bronze	Total
1	France	26	41	34	101
2	United States	19	14	14	47
3	Great Britain	15	6	9	30
4	Mixed Team	6	3	3	12
5	Switzerland	6	2	1	9
6	Belgium	5	5	5	15
7	Germany	4	2	2	8
8	Italy	2	1	0	3
9	Australia	2	0	3	5
10	Denmark	1	3	2	6

Whole new ball games

The programme for the 1936 Games in Berlin included men's Handball and Basketball tournaments. In the Basketball Final, the USA beat neighbours Canada 19–8 with the game played outdoors on a dirt pitch in heavy rain. As a result of the sodden surface, the players were unable to dribble with the ball, hence the low score, while the 1,000 spectators were forced to stand as the organisers did not provide any seating.

Greek Judokan champion

Ilias Iliadis won Greece's first ever gold medal in men's Judo when he claimed the 81kg title at Athens 2004.

The Thorpedo

At Sydney 2000, home favourite Ian Thorpe won the gold medal in the men's 400m Freestyle, breaking his own world record. The 17-year-old, nicknamed 'Thorpedo', then swam the anchor leg in the men's 4 x 100m Freestyle Relay and helped his country to gold. He claimed his third gold at the Games in the men's 4 x 200m Freestyle Relay and added a silver medal in the men's 200m Freestyle.

Weymouth and Portland

Weymouth Bay and Portland Harbour, situated in the county of Dorset on England's south coast, will be the venue for the Olympic and Paralympic Sailing competitions. It was the first venue for the London 2012 Games to be finished and comprises the Weymouth and Portland National Sailing Academy (WPNSA) and the adjoining commercial marina. The project has kick-started the regeneration of the former Naval Air Station at Portland, now known as Osprey Quay, where new residential, commercial and marina facilities are already under construction. Weymouth and Portland provides some of the best natural sailing waters in the UK, with facilities on land to match. The site has already hosted numerous international sailing events, including the 2006 ISAF World Youth Championships, which was attended by over 60 nations. The enhancements to the WPNSA sailing facilities include a new permanent 250m slipway and new lifting and mooring facilities. The project was completed on budget and ahead of schedule, providing world-class facilities for elite athletes and the local community more than three years before the Games. And the structures will remain in place after the Games, meaning that the United Kingdom's National Sailing Academy will benefit from the use of a world-class, state-of-the-art sailing facility for elite training, competition and local community use.

Finn plays second fiddle to Finn

Ville Ritola (Finland) won the men's 10,000m at the 1924 Olympic Games in Paris, breaking his own world record by 12 seconds in the process. He also won the men's 3000m Steeplechase – by 75 metres – the men's Cross-Country Team event and the men's 3000m Team event. He also claimed two silver medals, finishing behind his compatriot, Paavo Nurmi, in the men's 5000m and the men's Individual Cross-Country. In fact, Ritola was outshone by Nurmi, who won five gold medals at Paris 1924 and nine in his career.

Jesse Owens (1913–80)

1 James Cleveland (JC or Jesse) Owens was born on 12 September 1913 in Oakville, Alabama, USA.

2 When he was nine years old, his family migrated to Cleveland, Ohio, and he later attended the Ohio State University, though without a scholarship.

3 As a black student, he had to endure segregation, living off campus, staying at 'blacks only' hotels and eating in 'blacks only' restaurants.

4 On 25 May 1935, at the Big Ten college athletics meeting at Ann Arbor, Michigan, Owens broke three world records and tied a fourth, all in the space of 45 minutes.

5 He tied the 100 yards record and broke the long jump, 220 yards sprint and 220 yards low hurdles marks.

6 At the 1936 Olympic Games in Berlin, Owens won the men's 100m gold, just ahead of US team-mate Ralph Metcalfe. It was the only gold medal Adolf Hitler saw him win.

7 He went on to win gold medals in the men's Long Jump, men's 200m and men's 4 x 100m Relay – a feat that was matched by Carl Lewis 48 years later.

8 Although he was snubbed by Hitler, the German public adored him.

9 In America, Owens still encountered racism and observed, 'Hitler didn't snub me – it was FDR (US President Franklin Delano Roosevelt) who snubbed me. The president didn't even send me a telegram.'

10 Unlike the modern practice, as a champion athlete he was never invited to the White House.

11 He was stripped of his amateur status in 1937 and was forced to earn money racing in promotional events.

12 Jesse Owens died of lung cancer on 31 March 1980, aged 66, in Tucson, Arizona.

Did you know that?

The Jesse Owens Memorial Stadium, a multi-sport facility, was opened in 2001 on the Ohio State University campus.

Let the Games begin

The London 2012 Games will kick-off on 25 July, with the very first sporting action of the Games being the preliminary rounds of the women's Football at the Millennium Stadium in Cardiff.

Olympic Games talk (2)

'I declare the opening of the first international Olympic Games in Athens. Long live the Nation. Long live the Greek people.'
King George I *of Greece, opening the 1896 Games in Athens*

Peace to all

The 1920 Games at Antwerp were the first in which doves were released to symbolise peace. The Games came just two years after the end of the First World War, in which 28 countries had been involved and almost ten million soldiers had lost their lives in four years. In the scheduled four-year cycle of the Games, Berlin 1916 would have been the Games of the VI Olympiad and is still counted in the sequence, even though they were not held.

Upsetting the neighbours

At Atlanta 1996, Canada's quartet of Robert Esmie, Glenroy Gilbert, Bruny Surin and individual men's 100m gold-medal winner Donovan Bailey pulled off a big shock by beating the USA into second place in the men's 4 x 400m Relay.

The flying Kiwi

At Tokyo 1964, New Zealand's Peter Snell retained his title in the men's 800m and also claimed gold in the men's 1500m. Despite a relatively short career, which also saw him set five world records (800m, 800 yards, 1000m, 1500m and the mile) he was voted New Zealand's 'Sports Champion of the 20th Century'. It would be 41 years before Snell's men's 800m/1500m gold-medal double was equalled in open global championship, when Rashid Ramzi of Bahrain won both middle-distance events at the Helsinki 2005 IAAF Athletics World Championships.

The mighty Magyars

At the 1952 Games in Helsinki, Hungary's 'Magical Magyars' won the gold medal in the men's Football, defeating Yugoslavia 2–0 in the final. This was the team that played a then record 33 international games without defeat between 14 May 1950 and 4 July 1954. Hungary also won the Football gold medal at the 1964 Games in Tokyo and 1968 Games in Mexico City.

Youngest-ever gold medallist

At the 1932 Games in Los Angeles, 14-year-old Kusuo Kitamura of Japan won the men's 1500m Freestyle Swimming gold medal in a time of 19:12.40, to become the youngest male in any sport ever to win a gold medal in an individual event at the Games.

Back from the dead

The 1928 Olympic Games in Amsterdam broke new ground for female athletes. The 100m was the first women's track event to be contested and was won by Betty Robinson (USA) in a time equalling the then world record of 12.02 seconds. She also won a silver medal in the women's 4 x 100m Relay. Amazingly, Robinson had competed in her first 100m race only four months before the Games, and this was only the fourth track meet of her career. In her first outdoor track meeting, the 16-year-old American schoolgirl finished second to the USA record holder Elta Cartwright, and in her next race she equalled the world record for 100m, but her time was not officially recognised. In 1931, Robinson was so severely injured in a plane crash that the man who found her among the wreckage thought she was dead. He placed her body in the boot of his car and drove to the local mortuary – where the mortician discovered that she was still alive. Robinson remained unconscious for seven weeks and her injuries were so severe she could not walk normally for almost two years. Remarkably, Robinson still wanted to return to competitive sprinting, but the legacy of the injuries she sustained in the crash restricted the movement of her leg as she was unable to bend her leg fully at the knee. This meant that she could not take up the crouched starting position for the 100m. Undaunted by this, she concentrated on running in relays, and she came back from the dead to win a second gold medal as a member of the USA's women's 4 x 100m Relay team at the 1936 Games in Berlin.

First black Swimming gold medallist

Surinam's Anthony Nesty won his country's first-ever Olympic Games medal when he claimed gold in the men's 100m Butterfly at the 1988 Olympic Games in Seoul. He was not only the first black swimmer to win gold at the Games but also only the second black swimmer to win any medal at the Games, following Enith Sijtje Maria Brigitha (Netherlands), who won two bronze medals (women's 100m Freestyle and women's 200m Freestyle) at Montreal 1976.

The Olympic Oath

The Olympic Oath was composed by Baron Pierre de Coubertin, the founder of the modern Olympic Games. It was first taken by an athlete at the 1920 Games in Antwerp. The first Olympic Officials' Oath was taken at the 1972 Olympic Games in Munich. The wording of the Olympic Oath has altered slightly over the years. The one read by Victor Boin in 1920 was: 'We swear we will take part in the Olympic Games in a spirit of chivalry, for the honour of our country and for the glory of sport.' In subsequent years the word 'swear' was replaced by 'promise' and 'country' was replaced by 'team'. For the 2000 Games in Sydney, a reference to doping was included in the Oath. The athletes and judges who have delivered the Olympic Oath at the Olympic Games are as follows:

Games	Athletes' Olympic Oath	Judges' Oath
1920 Antwerp	Victor Boin	
1924 Paris	Georges Andre	
1928 Amsterdam	Harry Denis	
1932 Los Angeles	George Calnan	
1936 Berlin	Rudolf Ismayr	
1948 London	Don Finlay	
1952 Helsinki	Heikki Savolainen	
1956 Melbourne	John Landy	
	Henri Saint Cyr	
1960 Rome	Adolfo Consolini	
1964 Tokyo	Takashi Ono	
1968 Mexico City	Pablo Garrido	
1972 Munich	Heidi Schüller	Heinz Pollay
1976 Montreal	Pierre St-Jean	Maurice Fauget
1980 Moscow	Nikolay Andrianov	Aleksandr Medved
1984 Los Angeles	Edwin Moses	Sharon Weber
1988 Seoul	Hur Jae	Lee Hak-Rae
1992 Barcelona	Luis Doreste Blanco	Eugeni Asensio
1996 Atlanta	Teresa Edwards	Hobie Billingsly
2000 Sydney	Rechelle Hawkes	Peter Kerr
2004 Athens	Zoe Dimoschaki	Lazaros Voreadis
2008 Beijing	Zhang Yining	Huang Liping

Money-making venture

Total ticket revenues for the 1936 Games in Berlin amounted to 7.5 million marks, with a nominal profit in excess of 1 million marks.

St Louis 1904

On 1 July 1904, the Games of the III Olympiad were officially opened in St Louis, Missouri, by David Francis, President of the Louisiana Purchase Exposition at Francis Field (also known as the World's Fair). A total of 651 athletes (645 male, six female) from 12 different countries participated in 91 events across 17 sports. The Closing Ceremony was held on 23 November. Originally Chicago, Illinois, had bid successfully to host the 1904 Games, but the organizers of the Exposition refused to permit a rival event to take place at the same time. The organising committee behind the Exposition began to draw up a schedule of its own sporting events and wrote to the organising committee of the Chicago bid informing them that unless the Games were moved to St Louis the Exposition intended to overshadow the 1904 Olympic Games. President Theodore Roosevelt backed the St Louis bid, as the World's Fair was going to showcase the world's newest technologies, from automobiles to electricity. Eventually, Baron Pierre de Coubertin buckled under the pressure and Chicago lost out.

Final medals table (top ten)

Pos.	Nation	Gold	Silver	Bronze	Total
1	United States	78	82	79	239
2	Germany	4	4	5	13
3	Cuba	4	2	3	9
4	Canada	4	1	1	6
5	Hungary	2	1	1	4
6	Great Britain	1	1	0	2
	Mixed Team	1	1	0	2
8	Greece	1	0	1	2
	Switzerland	1	0	1	2
10	Austria	0	0	1	1

Student gold

Wyomia Tyus, a 19-year-old student from Tennessee State University, won the gold medal for the women's 100m at the 1964 Olympic Games in Tokyo, having equalled Wilma Rudolph's (USA) world record during her heats. She also claimed a silver in the women's 4 x 100m relay. She took the women's 100m gold four years later to become the first woman to win back-to-back 100m crowns. Tyus set a new world record in the women's 100m Final at Mexico City 1968 and also won gold in the women's 4 x 100m Relay.

London 2012 trailblazer

The London 2012 Olympic Torch was designed by east Londoners Edward Barber and Jay Osgerby. The Torch is made up of an inner and outer aluminium alloy skin, held in place by a cast top piece and base, perforated by 8,000 circles. Representing the inspirational stories of the 8,000 Torchbearers who will carry the Olympic Flame on its journey around the UK, the circles which run the length of the body of the Torch also offer a unique level of transparency. You can see right to the heart of the Torch and view the burner system which will keep the Olympic Flame alive. The Torch stands 800mm high, and its triangular shape was inspired by a series of 'threes' that are found in the Olympic Movement: the three Olympic values of respect, excellence and friendship; the three words that make the Olympic motto – faster, higher, stronger; and the fact that London has hosted the Olympic Games in 1908 and 1948 and will host them for a third time in 2012. Weighing just 800 grams, the Torch is specifically designed to be easily carried by the London 2012 Torchbearers, many of whom will be teenagers. Its gold colour embraces the qualities of the Olympic Flame – the brightness and warmth of the light that it shines.

Japanese runner goes missing

During the men's Marathon at Stockholm 1912, Japan's Shizo Kanakuri dropped out of the race near the town of Tureberg. He found a garden where he rested and was given refreshments by the owners of the house. The race officials were never informed that Kanakuri had withdrawn from the race, and Kanakuri only finished the race 55 years later when he ran into the Olympic Stadium during a visit to Stockholm in 1967.

East Germany's water babies

At the 1976 Games in Montreal, East Germany's women completely dominated the Swimming events, winning 11 of the 13 gold medals on offer. The only two events in the pool they lost were the women's 200m Backstroke, which was a 1–2–3 for the USSR, and the women's 4 x 100m Relay, which was won by the USA (East Germany took the silver). In total, the East German ladies won 11 golds, six silvers and one bronze. The East German men's Swimming team, meanwhile, managed only one medal from their 13 events – a bronze for Roland Matthes in the men's 100m Backstroke.

Olympic Games talk (3)

'I heard people yelling my name, and I couldn't realise how one fellow could have so many friends.'
Jim Thorpe, *double gold medallist at the 1912 Games in Stockholm, speaking about receiving a ticker-tape welcome on Broadway*

Olympic Games' first quad

At the 1900 Games in Paris, US athlete Alvin Christian Kraenzlein became the first sportsman to win four gold medals at a single Games and, more than 100 years later, he remains the only track and field athlete to achieve such a haul in individual events. Over the course of three days, Kraenzlein took the gold in the men's 60m, the men's 110m Hurdles, the men's 200m Hurdles and the men's Long Jump. In the men's 60m he ran both the preliminary round and the final in 7.0 seconds. His men's Long Jump victory, in which he defeated silver medallist Myer Prinstein by a single centimetre, was marred by controversy. Prinstein, the world record holder, had set his mark in the qualification round and, like his fellow American athletes, including Kraenzlein, he refused to compete in the final because it was being held on a Sunday. However, Kraenzlein changed his mind, and when Prinstein learned that Kraenzlein had not only competed, but had also beaten his mark, he became violent and reportedly punched Kraenzlein. In 1901, Kraenzlein, the holder of six world records, hung up his track shoes and concentrated on a career as an athletics coach.

Loser faster than the winner

At the 1984 Games in Los Angeles, two finals were introduced for the men's 400m Freestyle Swimming event. The eight fastest qualifiers took part in the 'A' Final and the next eight in a consolation 'B' Final. However, rather to the embarrassment of the organisers, the winner of the 'B' Final, Thomas Fahrner (West Germany), recorded a faster time than George Dicarlo (USA), the winner of the 'A' final. The two-final set-up was discontinued after Atlanta 1996.

All over before it started

The outdoor Tennis tournament at the 1912 Olympic Games in Stockholm started on 26 June and was completed one day before the Opening Ceremony.

Specially built stadia for the Games

The following stadia were specifically built to play host to the Olympic Games and include the words "Olympic Stadium" in their name:

Stockholms Olympiastadion – Stockholm (1912)
Olympisch Stadion – Antwerp (1920)
Stade Olympique de Colombes – Paris (1924)
Olympisch Stadion – Amsterdam (1928)
Olympiastadion – Berlin (1936)
Olympiastadion – Helsinki (1952)
Stadio Olimpico – Rome (1960)
Olympiastadion – Munich (1972)
Le Stade Olympique – Montreal (1976)
Centennial Olympic Stadium – Atlanta (1996)
Olympiako Stadio Athinas 'Spyros Louis' – Athens (2004)
Olympic Stadium – London (2012)

Three strikes and you're out

Baseball was voted out of the programme for the London 2012 Games at an IOC meeting on 7 July 2005, becoming the first sport to be voted out of the Games since Polo was withdrawn from the Berlin 1936 Games.

Lasse the Great

On lap 12 (of 25) of the men's 10,000m Final at Munich 1972, Lasse Viren of Finland fell over. He quickly got back to his feet and went on to claim the gold medal and break Ron Clarke's seven-year-old world record for the distance. Viren's winning time was 27:38.40. Viren also won gold in the men's 5000m to become only the fourth athlete in history to win the men's 5,000m-10,000m double. Four years later, at Montreal 1976, Viren won both events again, becoming the first man to repeat as winner of the men's 5000m at the Games. Amazingly, just 18 hours after winning the men's 5000m Final at Munich 1972, he competed in the men's Marathon and finished in a highly respectable fifth place, clocking a time of 2:13.11. Viren's career at the Games ended at Moscow 1980 when he could manage only fifth place in the men's 10,000m and was outclassed by Miruts Yifter and the rest of the pack in the men's 5000m. In addition to the men's 10,000m, Viren also broke the world record at both two miles and 5000m.

The parade of the delegations

During the Opening Ceremony at the 1908 Games in London at the newly built White City Stadium, the athletes marched into the stadium by nation, as most countries sent selected national teams. This was the first time athletes had been paraded in sports uniforms walking behind the flag of their nation at the start of an Olympic Games, a tradition that was followed in subsequent Games and became known as the Parade of the Delegations (or Nations). However, in 1908, the infamous 'Battle of Shepherd's Bush' occurred when the delegation from the USA noticed that there was no American flag among the national flags decorating the stadium for the Opening Ceremony. Martin Sheridan, winner of the men's Discus Throw gold medal at St Louis 1904 and the 1908 Flag Bearer for the USA, responded by refusing to dip the Stars and Stripes when he passed King Edward VII's box. 'This flag dips to no earthly King,' said Sheridan, who was born in Treenduff, County Mayo, Ireland, and who would go on to take gold in the men's Discus Throw and the men's Greek Discus Throw events at the Games. However, the US athletes were not the only ones to have a complaint over the flags. At the time, the Grand Duchy of Finland was ruled by Russia, but when the Finnish athletes were informed that they would have to march into the stadium behind Russia's 'hammer and sickle' flag, they refused and elected to march with no flag at all. Similarly, Irish athletes were compelled to compete for the British team, and many of them withdrew from the Ceremony altogether rather than march behind the Union Jack. Meanwhile, the Swedish flag had not been displayed above the stadium and, consequently, the members of the Swedish team also decided not to take part in the Opening Ceremony. Although the custom is to dip the nation's flag as a sign of respect to heads of state attending the cermony, since 1908 USA flag bearers have followed Sheridan's example by not doing so.

1956 Games boycott

Two international incidents resulted in six countries boycotting the 1956 Games in Melbourne. As a direct result of the Suez Crisis, Egypt, Iraq and Lebanon declined their invitation to compete at the Games, and the Soviet Union's invasion of Hungary led to the withdrawal of the Netherlands, Spain and Switzerland. In addition, less than two weeks before the Opening Ceremony, the People's Republic of China also withdrew from the Games because the Republic of China (under the name Formosa) had been permitted to compete.

London 2012 Olympic venues

Olympic Stadium Athletics • Opening and Closing Ceremonies

Aquatics Centre Diving • Modern Pentathlon • Paralympic Swimming • Swimming • Synchronised Swimming

Basketball Arena Basketball • Wheelchair Basketball • Wheelchair Rugby • Handball

BMX Track BMX Cycling

City of Coventry Stadium Football

Earls Court Volleyball

Eton Dorney Canoe Sprint • Paralympic Rowing • Rowing

Eton Manor Wheelchair Tennis

ExCeL Boccia • Boxing • Fencing • Judo • Paralympic Table Tennis • Paralympic Judo • Paralympic Powerlifting • Table Tennis • Taekwondo • Volleyball (Sitting) • Weightlifting • Wheelchair Fencing • Wrestling

Greenwich Park Equestrian (Jumping, Dressage and Eventing) • Modern Pentathlon • Paralympic Equestrian

Hadleigh Farm Cycling – Mountain Bike

Hampden Park Football

Hampton Court Road Cycling (Time Trial)

Handball Arena Goalball • Handball • Modern Pentathlon

Hockey Centre Hockey • Paralympic Five-a-side Football • Paralympic Seven-a-side Football

Horse Guards Parade Beach Volleyball

Hyde Park Swimming – Marathon • Triathlon

Lee Valley White Water Centre Canoe Slalom

Lord's Cricket Ground Archery

The Mall Athletics – Marathon and Race Walk • Paralympic Athletics (Marathon) • Road Cycling

Millennium Stadium Football

North Greenwich Arena Basketball • Gymnastics – Artistic • Trampoline • Wheelchair Basketball

Old Trafford Football

The Royal Artillery Barracks Paralympic Archery • Paralympic Shooting • Shooting

St James' Park Football

Velodrome Cycling – Track • Paralympic Track Cycling

Water Polo Arena Water Polo

Wembley Arena Badminton • Gymnastics – Rhythmic

Wembley Stadium Football

Weymouth and Portland Paralympic Sailing • Sailing

Wimbledon Tennis

London 1908

The 1908 Olympic Games in London were officially opened on 27 April 1908 by HRH King Edward VII. The Games had originally been awarded to Rome, but were reassigned to London following an eruption of Mount Vesuvius, near Naples, on 7 April 1906. The Italian government needed money for urgent rebuilding in the disaster zone and appealed to the IOC for the Games to be given to another city. The other two candidate cities who lost out to Rome to host the 1908 Games, Berlin and Milan, did not think they could organise the event at only 18 months' notice. However, despite the lack of time, London's offer to host the Games was accepted by the IOC in November 1906. As it turned out, although the Games were held in conjunction with the Franco-British Exhibition, which at the time was a better-known event than the Olympic Games, London 1908 was the best-organised Games to date. The organisation was helped greatly by the fact that many of the governing bodies of sports in Britain had already been in existence for many years. A total of 22 nations sent 2,008 athletes (1,971 men, 37 women) to participate in 110 events across 22 sports. The Closing Ceremony took place on 31 October 1908.

Final medals table (top ten)

Pos.	Nation	Gold	Silver	Bronze	Total
1	Great Britain	56	51	38	145
2	United States	23	12	12	47
3	Sweden	8	6	11	25
4	France	5	5	9	19
5	Germany	3	5	6	14
6	Hungary	3	4	2	9
7	Canada	3	3	10	16
8	Norway	2	3	3	8
9	Italy	2	2	0	4
10	Belgium	1	5	2	8

Record medal haul

Aleksandr Dityatin (USSR) won eight medals in the eight Gymnastics events he contested at Moscow 1980. His medal haul was a then record for a single Games. At his first Games, Montreal 1976, he won two silver medals, in the men's Rings and the Team competitions. Dityatin's medal haul at a single Games has since been equalled by swimmer Michael Phelps at both Athens 2004 and Beijing 2008.

Four-week games introduced

The 1932 Games in Los Angeles were the shortest to date, lasting 16 days. Between Paris 1900 and Amsterdam 1928, no Games lasted less than 79 days. Since 1932, no Games has lasted longer than 18 days. The 1896 Olympic Games in Athens lasted only nine days.

America's Swimming queen

America's Amy Van Dyke won four gold medals at the Atlanta 1996 Games (50m Freestyle, 100m Butterfly, 4 x 100m Freestyle Relay and 4 x 100m Medley Relay. Her haul made her the first female American to win four gold medals in a single Games. She also won gold medals in the same two Swimming Relays at Sydney 2004.

GDR cleans up in the water

At the 1980 Olympic Games in Moscow, the East German ladies repeated their domination in the Swimming, again winning 11 of the 13 gold medals on offer. Only Australia's Michelle Ford (women's 800m Freestyle) and the USSR's Lina Kaciusyte (women's 200m Breaststroke) prevented a clean sweep of gold medals for the GDR. They were so good that they completed a 1-2-3 in six events, and claimed 26 of the 35 medals available (they won the gold medal in the two relay races, where only one team per country competes). On the East German men's Swimming team, only Jorg Woithe won a gold medal, in the men's 100m Freestyle. The GDR were equally dominant in the Rowing events, winning 11 of the 14 gold medals. Their men won seven out of eight events and were only denied a clean sweep by Finland's Pertti Karppinen, who retained his men's Single Sculls title, while the women won four of their six events.

Dramatic men's Marathon finish

The men's Marathon at the 1948 Olympic Games in London had a dramatic finish as Belgium's Etienne Gailly entered Wembley Stadium in first place with just 400 metres of the race left. However, Gailly was so exhausted he could barely stay on his feet. He was overtaken by Argentina's Delfo Cabrera, who won the gold medal, and also by Great Britain's Thomas Richards, who took the silver. Gailly managed to cross the line – without assistance – to win the bronze. The finish to the race was reminiscent of Dorando Pietri's tragic near miss in the men's Marathon at the 1908 Games in London.

Olympic Games talk (4)

'Scientists have proven that it's impossible to long-jump 30 feet, but I don't listen to that kind of talk. Thoughts like that have a way of sinking into your feet.'
Carl Lewis, *who never made a 30ft (9.14-metre) long jump, but won Olympic Games gold medals in 1984, 1988, 1992 and 1996*

The world's fastest sprinter

Canada's Donovan Bailey became the world's fastest man when he won the men's 100m gold medal at Atlanta 1996 in a new world record time of 9.84 seconds. The record has been broken many times since, by American Maurice Greene in 1999 (9.79), twice by Jamaican Asafa Powell, in 2005 (9.77) and 2007 (9.74) and three times by Usain Bolt, at Beijing in 2008 (9.72 and 9.69) and in 2009 (9.58).

Global unity down under

Prior to the 1956 Olympic Games in Melbourne, the athletes marched into the stadium at the Closing Ceremony by nation, just as they did in the Opening Ceremony. However, this protocol was set aside in 1956, when John Ian Wing, a young Australian, suggested to the Australian IOC that the athletes enter the stadium for the Closing Ceremony together as a symbol of global unity. In his letter to the Australian NOC, Wing wrote: 'During the Games there will be only one nation. War, politics and nationalities will be forgotten. What more could anybody want if the world could be made one nation.'

Braveheart

At the 1952 Games in Helsinki, Danish Equestrian star Lis Hartel won a silver medal in the Individual Dressage. Prior to Helsinki 1952, the Dressage competition at the Games was only open to men, so it was the first time she had been allowed to enter. Hartel's triumph was even more amazing because she had contracted polio in 1944 and, although she had regained the use of most of her muscles, she remained paralysed below the knees and had to be helped on and off her horse, Jubilee. A keen horsewoman, Hartel finished second in the Scandinavian Riding Championships to earn her place in the Danish team for the 1952 Games. Hartel and Jubilee went on to win a second silver medal at the 1956 Games in Melbourne.

Women's 100m Fantasy Olympic Games Final

Lane No./Athlete	Country	Medals
1 Stanislawa Walasiewicz	Poland	Gold – Los Angeles 1932, Silver – Berlin 1936
2 Wyomia Tyus	USA	2 Gold – Tokyo 1964 and Mexico City 1968
3 Fanny Blankers-Koen	Netherlands	Gold – London 1948
4 Renate Stecher	E. Germany	Gold – Munich 1972, Silver – Montreal 1976
5 Gail Devers	USA	2 Gold – Barcelona 1992 and Atlanta 1996
6 Pauline Davis-Thompson	Bahamas	Gold – Sydney 2000, Silver – Atlanta 1996
7 Evelyn Ashford	USA	Gold – Los Angeles 1984, Silver – Seoul 1988
8 Betty Cuthbert	Australia	Gold – Melbourne 1956

Jim Thorpe (1888 – 1953)

1 Jim Thorpe was born on a Sac and Fox American Indian reservation in Oklahoma, USA, on 28 May 1888.

2 His American-Indian name, Wa-Tho-Huck, translates as Bright Path.

3 A multi-talented athlete, not only in track and field, he also played baseball, American football, lacrosse and basketball.

4 Before going to Stockholm for the 1912 Olympic Games, he was the inter-collegiate ballroom dancing champion.

5 At the 1912 Olympic Games in Stockholm, he won the men's Pentathlon and men's Decathlon golds – a unique achievement.

6 King Gustav V of Sweden said to him at the Victory Ceremony, 'You, sir, are the greatest athlete in the world.' Thorpe replied, 'Thanks, King.'

7 After his exploits as a semi-pro baseball player came to light in 1913, he was stripped of his Olympic Games medals.

8 Free to turn to professional sport, he played baseball and American football and led barnstorming basketball tours.

9 When the precursor of American football's NFL, the APFA, began life in 1920, Thorpe was named as its first president, even though he continued to play in the league.

10 Jim Thorpe suffered poverty and cancer in later life and died on 28 March 1953, in Lomita, California.

11 In 1950, he was named the greatest athlete of the half-century; in 1999, he was third in the Associated Press's athlete of the century rankings.

12 In 1983, 30 years after Jim Thorpe's death, the IOC returned his medals to his family.

Did you know that?
The Jim Thorpe Museum and Oklahoma Hall of Fame is in Oklahoma City, the state of his birth. The Jim Thorpe Association and Bright Path Youth Programme help to fund children and young adults through school and university, providing scholarships.

Eric the Eel

Eric Moussambani from Equatorial Guinea learned how to swim in January 2000 and went to the 2000 Games in Sydney as a wildcard entry. He had never ever seen a 50-metre pool before and finished more than one minute outside the Olympic Games record in the men's 100m Freestyle. He was quickly nicknamed 'Eric the Eel'.

The Water Cube

The Beijing National Aquatics Centre, also known as 'The Water Cube', was constructed alongside the National Stadium in the Olympic Forest Park. This showcase arena, which staged the Swimming, Diving and Synchronised Swimming events at the 2008 Games, has an avant-garde structural design inspired by research done into the natural formation of soap bubbles. The Water Polo and the Modern Pentathlon's swimming discipline were originally due to be held there too, but were staged in the Ying Tung Natatorium.

German propaganda

The German government saw the 1936 Olympic Games in Berlin as the ideal opportunity to promote their Nazi ideology. The IOC commissioned Leni Riefenstahl, one of Hitler's favourite film-makers, to film the 1936 Games. Riefenstahl's film was called *Olympia* and the techniques she employed have served as an inspiration to sports movie-makers ever since. Riefenstahl opted to highlight the aesthetics of the body by filming it from every angle.

Cross-Channel Swimming gold

At the 1924 Games in Paris, US swimmer Gertrude Ederle won a gold medal in the women's 4 x 100m Freestyle Relay and bronze medals in the women's 100m and 400m Freestyle events. Two years later she caused a worldwide sensation by not only becoming the first woman to swim across the English Channel, but also doing so in a time almost two hours faster than any man had ever achieved. Her historic and record-breaking cross-Channel swim began at 7.05am on 6 August 1926 from Cap Gris-Nez, France, and, 14 hours 30 minutes later, she came ashore at Kingsdown, England. Her record stood for 24 years, until Florence Chadwick swam the Channel in 13 hours 20 minutes on 8 August 1950.

Triathlon makes its debut

The Triathlon made its debut at the Games at Sydney 2000. The event began in the picturesque surroundings of the Sydney Opera House. Switzerland's Brigitte McMahon won the women's event and Canada's Simon Whitfield was the men's gold medallist. Athletes from five nations collected medals, with Switzerland claiming two – Magali Messmer won bronze in the women's competition.

Stockholm 1912

The 1912 Games in Stockholm, the Games of the V Olympiad, were opened on 5 May 1912 by HRH King Gustav V. The most efficiently run Games to date, dubbed 'The Swedish Masterpiece', the Games witnessed the introduction of unofficial electronic timing devices for the track events, a photo-finish machine and the first use of a public address system. The 1912 Games also had several new events added to the programme, including the Modern Pentathlon, Equestrian events and women's events in Swimming and Diving. A total of 28 nations sent 2,407 athletes (2,359 men, 48 women) to participate in 102 events across 14 sports. The Closing Ceremony took place on 27 July 1912.

Final medals table (top ten)

Pos.	Nation	Gold	Silver	Bronze	Total
1	United States	25	19	19	63
2	Sweden	24	24	17	65
3	Great Britain	10	15	16	41
4	Finland	9	8	9	26
5	France	7	4	3	14
6	Germany	5	13	7	25
7	South Africa	4	2	0	6
8	Norway	4	1	4	9
9	Canada	3	2	3	8
	Hungary	3	2	3	8

First home television Games

The 1948 Games in London were the first to be shown on home television, although the viewing figures were low. The reason for this is that very few people in Britain actually owned television sets.

Backing the Soviets

A total of 14 countries took part in the Soviet-led boycott of the 1984 Olympic Games in Los Angeles:

Afghanistan • Angola • Bulgaria • Cuba • Czechoslovakia
East Germany • Ethiopia • Hungary • Laos • Mongolia
North Korea • Poland • USSR • Vietnam

Iran and Libya also boycotted the Games, citing political reasons other than support for the Soviets.

IOC Presidents from 1894 to present

Period	Name	Country
1894–1896	Demetrius Vikelas	Greece
1896–1925	Baron Pierre de Coubertin	France
1925–1942	Count Henri de Baillet-Latour	Belgium
1946–1952	J. Sigfrid Edstrom	Sweden
1952–1972	Avery Brundage	USA
1972–1980	Lord Killanin	Great Britain
1980–2001	Juan Antonio Samaranch	Spain
2001–	Jacques Rogge	Belgium

Big red machine rules the pool

In the men's Swimming competition at Barcelona 1992, Unified Team (former USSR) swimmers dominated the Freestyle events, winning the 50m, 100m, 200m, 400m and 4 x 200m Relay. They failed to win the 1500m, won by Australia's Kieren Perkins, and the 4 x 100m Relay, which the USA won from the Unified Team. Alexander Popov and Evgueni Sadovyi won two gold medals each in individual events, while Sadovyi claimed a third in the 4 x 200m Relay.

All on her own

Annegret Richter (West Germany), who won the women's 100m at Montreal 1976, was the only female athlete from outside Eastern Europe to win a gold medal on the track at the Games. East Germany's women won nine of the 14 track and field golds (with two going to the USSR and one each to Bulgaria and Poland) and made a clean sweep of the medal places in the women's Pentathlon.

Political games down under

In the lead-up to the 1956 Games in Melbourne, Australian politicians were divided over the cost to the country of hosting an Olympic Games. The Premier of Victoria refused to allocate funds to build an Olympic Village in Melbourne, as there was a shortage of housing for the local population. The Olympic Village was eventually constructed in Heidelberg West, a suburb of Melbourne. The Australian Prime Minister also stated that federal funds could not be used to pay for the costs of hosting the Games. IOC President Avery Brundage became so impatient with the political in-fighting that he almost awarded the 1956 Games to Rome instead.

An act of sportsmanship

During the Sailing compeitition at the 1988 Games in Seoul, Lawrence Lemieux (Canada) was in second place in the fifth of a seven-race Finn class and looking good to claim a silver medal when he abandoned the race to save two men. First he rescued Singapore's Joseph Chan and then sailed towards another Singapore sailor, Shaw Her Siew, who was clinging to his overturned boat. Lemieux waited for an official patrol boat to reach him and take the two sailors ashore before continuing in his event. However, his 22nd-place finish in the race ended his hopes of a medal. Shortly after the completion of the Finn class races, the International Yacht Racing Union unanimously decided that Lemieux should be awarded second place in the fifth race, a decision none of the other contestants questioned. Although Lemieux did not win a medal, he was awarded the Pierre de Coubertin Medal for Sportsmanship. 'By your sportsmanship, self-sacrifice and courage you embody all that is right with the Olympic Ideal,' said the IOC President Juan Antonio Samaranch.

Long's Long Jump advice

At the 1936 Games in Berlin, Jesse Owens won four gold medals, one of which was in the men's Long Jump event. Much to the dissatisfaction of the German officials, his German rival, Carl Ludwig 'Lutz' Long, gave Owens advice on his technique after he almost failed to qualify for the final. Long had actually set a new Games record during his qualifying round, but Owens bettered Long's distance in the final to claim the gold medal. Long was the first to congratulate Owens, and the pair walked arm in arm to the dressing-room. Following his death on 13 July 1943, Long was posthumously awarded the Pierre de Coubertin medal for sportsmanship. 'It took a lot of courage for him to befriend me in front of Hitler,' said Owens about Long's congratulations. 'You can melt down all the medals and cups I have and they wouldn't be plating on the twenty-four kilates friendship that I felt for Lutz Long at that moment.'

Olympic Games talk (5)

'The efficiency and almost mathematical precision with which the events were handled and the formal correctness of the arrangements made a great impression on me.'
American **Avery Brundage**, the IOC President from 1952 to 1972, describing the 1912 Olympic Games in Stockholm

Olympic Mascots

The 1968 Games in Mexico City saw the IOC introduce an official mascot. Since then, each Games has had its own mascot(s):

Mexico City 1968
An unnamed red jaguar.

Munich 1972
Waldi, a dachshund dog, chosen to represent the attributes required for athletes – resistance, tenacity and agility. Designer: Otl Aicher.

Montreal 1976
Amik, a beaver, one of Canada's national symbols.

Moscow 1980
Misha, a bear cub, designed by children's books illustrator Victor Chizhikov.

Los Angeles 1984
Sam the Eagle, a bald eagle, one of the symbols of the USA, designed by Robert Moore from the Walt Disney Company.

Seoul 1988
Hodori and Hosuni, two tigers (Hodori is a male cub, Hosuni female), two of Korea's legends. Designer: Hyum Kim.

Barcelona 1992
Cobi, a Cubist Catalan sheepdog. Designer: Javier Marischal.

Atlanta 1996
Izzy, an abstract figure whose name was changed from Whatizit (i.e. What is it?).

Sydney 2000
Olly, a kookaburra, representing the Games' spirit of generosity; the name derives from 'Olympic'. Syd, a platypus, representing the environment and the energy of the Australian people. Syd's name derives from Sydney. Millie, an echidna representing the millennium.

Athens 2004
Athena and Phevos, brother and sister, two modern children resembling ancient Greek dolls. Designer: Spyros Gogos.

Beijing 2008
The *Fuwa*, comprising of five figures: *Beibei*, a fish; *Jingjing*, a giant panda; *Huanhuan*, the Olympic Flame; *Yingying*, a Tibetan antelope; and *Nini*, a swallow.

London 2012
Wenlock and Mandeville, fashioned from drops of steel used in the construction of the Olympic Stadium and named after British towns Much Wenlock in Shropshire (a venue for a mid-nineteenth-century games, similar to the Olympic Games) and Stoke Mandeville in Buckinghamshire (the original home of the Paralympic Games).

Black Power salute

In the final of the men's 200m at Mexico City 1968, Tommie Smith of the USA won the gold medal, Peter Norman of Australia the silver and Smith's team-mate, John Carlos, the bronze. Smith won the race in a new world record time of 19.83 seconds. However, it was the Victory Ceremony that followed that stands out as one of the most defining moments in the history of the modern Olympic Games. Both Smith and Carlos walked on to the podium shoeless (they wore black socks to represent black poverty) and when 'The Star Spangled Banner', the US national anthem, was played, they both bowed their heads and gave the Black Power salute. Smith and Carlos made the gesture to protest at the blatant discrimination against blacks in America. All three athletes on the podium wore OPHR (Olympic Project for Human Rights) badges, while Smith also wore a black scarf around his neck and Carlos a set of black beads. It was Norman who had suggested that Smith and Carlos wear one glove each when it emerged that Carlos had forgotten his pair – Smith wore the right one and Carlos the left. A number of IOC officials, notably the President, Avery Brundage, believed that their protest was a political statement that had no place at an Olympic Games. Both Smith and Carlos were thrown off the US team by the United States Olympic Committee (USOC) and banned from the Olympic Village. They also received lifetime bans from the Games. However, many people praised the two athletes for their bravery in taking a stance against racism in the USA, and Germany's Martin Jellinghaus, winner of the bronze medal in the men's 4 x 400m Relay, wore an OPHR badge in support of Smith and Carlos. Interviewed after the most famous civil rights protest in the Games' history, Smith said: 'If I win, I am American, not a black American. But if I did something bad, then they would say I am a Negro. We are black and we are proud of being black. Black America will understand what we did tonight.'

Peruvian withdrawal

Peru beat Austria 4–2 after extra time in the quarter-finals of the men's Football tournament at the 1936 Games in Berlin. However, a rematch was ordered when Austria claimed that the pitch was too small for competitive football matches and that the Peruvian fans had stormed the field after the fourth goal was scored. The Peruvian government regarded this as an insult and ordered their team to withdraw in protest. The Austrians went through, but Italy won the gold medal with Austria taking silver and Norway bronze.

Greco-Roman hat-trick

Swedish wrestler Carl Westergren won his third men's Greco-Roman Wrestling title during the 1932 Olympic Games in Los Angeles when he claimed gold in the Heavyweight (+87kg) division. Amazingly, he won his three gold medals in three different divisions. At Antwerp 1920, he won at Middleweight (67.5–75kg) and, at Paris 1924, he claimed the Light-Heavyweight (75–82.5kg) event. Westergren's compatriot, Ivar Johansson, a policeman, won gold medals in both Freestyle (Middleweight, 72–79kg) and Greco-Roman Wrestling (Welterweight, 66–72kg) at the same Games.

St Louis mirrors Paris confusion

Just as the events at the 1900 Games in Paris were relegated to sideshow activities in comparison to the events forming the 1900 World's Fair, held simultaneously in the French capital, St Louis followed a similarly confused path. As had been the case at Paris 1900, the 1904 Games in St Louis were held over a period of five months, and James Edward Sullivan, principal organiser of the Games, even attempted to hold an event every day for the duration of the fair. Once again the Games were intertwined with other sporting events, but unlike 1900, when the term 'Olympic' was rarely used to describe a competition, Sullivan gave all his events the 'Olympic' label. In a number of the events, the US National Championship was combined with the Olympic Games championship because there were no competitors from other nations to compete in the sport. Indeed, of the 651 athletes, 525 of them were American, and only 42 of the 91 events included athletes who were not from the USA.

Hadleigh Farm

Hadleigh Farm in Essex is the venue for the Mountain Bike course at the 2012 Games in London. The site is owned by the Salvation Army and covers 550 acres, which includes beautiful grassland and woodland.

First Olympic Games champion in 1,503 years

On the opening day of the 1896 Games in Athens, on 6 April, James Connolly (USA) won the men's Triple Jump to become the first Olympic Games champion for 1,503 years. He also finished second in the men's High Jump and third in the men's Long Jump. He also took part in the Paris 1900 Games, during which he claimed a second bronze.

Antwerp 1920

The 1920 Olympic Games in Antwerp were officially opened on 20 April 1920 by the Belgian monarch, His Majesty King Albert. The previous Games – those of the VI Olympiad – had been scheduled for Berlin in 1916, but the First World War caused them to be cancelled. The IOC awarded the next Games to Belgium to pay tribute to the suffering endured by the Belgian people during the War (the VI Olympiad was the first lost Olympiad). The 1920 Games witnessed two milestones: the Olympic Flag (created by Baron de Coubertin), with the five Olympic Rings signifying the union of five continents, was first flown there; and the Olympic Oath was first spoken there by Victor Boin, who represented the host nation in Fencing and Water Polo.

The outstanding competitor of the Games was Italy's Nedo Nadi, who claimed five of the six gold medals in the men's Fencing events. Oscar Swahn, a Swedish shooter aged 72, won a silver medal in the Team Double-shot Running Deer event to become the oldest medallist in the Games' history. On her way to winning the gold medal in all three women's Swimming contests, Ethelda Bleibtrey (USA) swam in five races, including preliminary heats, and broke the world record in every one. A total of 29 nations sent 2,626 athletes (2,561 men, 65 women) to participate in 154 events across 22 sports. The Closing Ceremony took place on 12 September 1920.

Final medals table (top ten)

Pos.	Nation	Gold	Silver	Bronze	Total
1	United States	41	27	27	95
2	Sweden	19	18	24	61
3	Great Britain	15	15	13	43
4	Finland	15	10	9	34
5	Belgium	14	11	11	36
6	Norway	13	9	9	31
7	Italy	13	5	5	23
8	France	9	19	13	41
9	Netherlands	4	2	5	11
10	Denmark	3	9	1	13

Tour de France winner claims gold

At the 1996 Games in Atlanta, professional cyclists were allowed to enter for the first time. Spain's Miguel Indurain, five times winner of the Tour de France, won the inaugural Individual Time Trial event.

The Fosbury Flop

Richard 'Dick' Fosbury won the men's High Jump gold medal at Mexico City 1968 with his innovative 'Fosbury Flop' technique, setting a new Games record of 2.24 metres (7ft 4¼in). Whereas most high jumpers used the Californian western roll or straddle, Fosbury sprinted diagonally towards the bar, then curved and leapt backwards over it. After the Games, the Californian western roll was a thing of the past.

Summon the heroes

The official theme music of the 1996 Games in Atlanta was 'Summon the Heroes', by John Williams, his third composition at a Games. However, the official song of the 1996 Games was 'Reach', which was sung by Gloria Estefan at the Closing Ceremony.

Double double East German gold

At the 1980 Olympic Games in Moscow, East Germany's Waldemar Cierpinski retained his men's Marathon gold medal, while his compatriot Barbel Wockel won the women's 200m gold to become the first female athlete to successfully defend this title.

Male wins women's 100m gold

Poland's Stanislawa Walasiewicz won the women's 100m gold medal at the 1932 Games in Los Angeles. The 21-year-old Pole equalled the world record of 11.9 seconds in her heat and then recorded the same blistering time in the final. Later the same day, she finished sixth in the women's Discus Throw. When she returned to Poland, a huge number of fans turned out to greet her arrival in the port of Gdynia, and a few days later she was presented with the golden 'Cross of Merit', a medal awarded in recognition of her services to the State. Four years later, she claimed the silver medal in the 100m at Berlin 1936. Walasiewicz later moved to America and took the name Stella Walsh. Following her death on 4 December 1980, killed as an innocent bystander in an armed robbery, an autopsy on her body revealed that she possessed male genitalia. Subsequently there were calls for all of her achievements and records to be stricken from the record books, but this was something neither the IOC nor the IAAF implemented. During her career, Walasiewicz set over 100 national and world records, including 51 Polish records, 18 world records and eight European records.

James Bond at the Sydney 2000 Games

In the James Bond film *Die Another Day*, Verity (played by Madonna) claims that the Miranda Frost character won a gold medal in women's Fencing at the 2000 Olympic Games in Sydney.

The Roy Jones controversy

In the final of Boxing's Light Middle Weight division (up to 71 kilograms) at the 1988 Games in Seoul, the red-hot favourite to win the gold medal, Roy Jones Jr of the USA, was beaten by home fighter, Park Si-Hun. Jones controversially lost the fight 3–2, leading to allegations that South Korean officials had rigged the judging. Many experts considered Jones as the true champion as he had absolutely battered his opponent over the three rounds, landing 86 punches to Park's 32. After the Boxing tournament ended, Jones was awarded the Val Barker trophy as the best stylistic boxer of the Games. Shortly after the fight ended, one of the judges admitted that the decision was a mistake, and all three judges who voted for Si-Hun were subsequently suspended. Nine years later, the IOC published the official report into the incident, in which it was revealed that three of the judges were wined and dined by South Korean officials. However, it was nine years too late for Jones and, surprisingly, the IOC did not overturn the result. The incident, coupled with another hotly disputed decision awarded in favour of Ivailo Marinov (Bulgaria) against the USA's Michael Carbajal in the Light Fly Weight event (up to 48 kg) at the same Games, resulted in the IOC creating a new scoring system for Boxing at the Olympic Games.

Hong Kong gold

Lee Lai Shan made history at Atlanta 1996 by winning Hong Kong's first ever gold medal when she won the women's Sailboard (Mistral) event.

Brothers Abrahams

Sidney Solomon 'Solly' Abrahams competed at the 1906 Intercalated Games in Athens, finishing fifth in the men's Long Jump. At Stockholm 1912 he finished 11th in the same event. He later served as Chief Justice of Ceylon (now Sri Lanka) from 1936–39, but Solly was not the greatest Olympian in his family: his younger brother, Harold Abrahams, won the men's 100m gold medal at Paris 1924, a race that was made more famous by the *Chariots of Fire* movie.

Olympic Games talk (6)

'Such is the power of a good "story" that for every thousand people who know Dorando's name, not even one is probably able to say who officially won the London Marathon.'

Harold Abrahams, *1924 gold medallist, on Dorando Pietri's disqualification in the men's Marathon at the London 1908 Games*

Cuban ring masters

In the Boxing competition at Moscow 1980, Cuba won six gold, two silver and two bronze medals from the 11 weight divisions. The only division in which they missed out on a podium place was Fly Weight. This impressive haul equalled the Games record, which had stood since St Louis 1904, when the USA won 11 Boxing medals on home soil. The Cubans' achievement was considerably greater, however, because in 1904 there were few contestants from outside the USA.

Seven into ten

Romania's Nadia Comaneci recorded seven perfect scores of ten in the Gymnastics competition at Montreal 1976. However, as no gymnast had ever achieved the perfect score before, and the scoreboard could actually display only three digits, her maximum marks were shown as '1.00'.

First female athletes

Madame Brohy and Mademoiselle Ohnier were the first women to participate at the Olympic Games when they represented France at Croquet at Paris 1900.

Jumping to glory

At the 1964 Games in Tokyo Mary Rand became the first British female athlete to win an Olympic Games gold medal in a track and field event when she won the women's Long Jump Final. She won the gold medal with a new world record leap of 6.76 metres, and today a plaque can be found in the Market Place of her hometown, Wells, Somerset, commemorating her achievement. She also won a silver medal in the women's Pentathlon and a bronze in the women's 4 x 100m Relay at the same Games. At the end of 1964, Rand won the BBC Sports Personality of the Year Award and, in 1965, was awarded an MBE.

Men's 200m fantasy Olympic Games Final

Lane No./Athlete	Country	Medals
1 Jesse Owens	USA	Gold – Berlin 1936
2 Usain Bolt	Jamaica	Gold – Beijing 2008
3 Carl Lewis	USA	Gold – Los Angeles 1984, Silver – Seoul 1988
4 Pietro Mennea	Italy	Gold – Moscow 1980, Bronze – Munich 1972
5 Michael Johnson	USA	Gold – Atlanta 1996
6 Bobby Kerr	Canada	Gold – London 1908
7 Don Quarrie	Jamaica	Gold – Montreal 1976
8 Andy Stanfield	USA	Gold – Helsinki 1952, Silver – Melbourne 1956

Notable achievements at the Games

Most medals
Men: 15: Nikolai Andrianov (USSR), Gymnastics, 1972–80
Women: 18: Larysa Latynina (USSR), Gymnastics, 1956–64

Most gold medals in individual events
Men: 8: Ray Ewry (USA), Athletics, 1900–08
Women: 7: Vera Caslavska (Cze), Gymnastics, 1964–68

Most consecutive victories in an individual event
Men: 4: Paul Elvstrom (Den), Finn class, Sailing, 1948–60
Al Oerter (USA), Discus Throw, 1956–68
Carl Lewis (USA), Long Jump, 1984–96
Women: 3: Larysa Latynina (USSR), Floor competition, 1956–64
Dawn Fraser (Aus) 100m Freestyle, 1956–64
Krisztina Egerszegi (Hun) 200m Backstroke, 1988–96

Most consecutive victories in same event, Team
6: Aladar Gerevich (Hun), Team Sabre, Fencing, 1932–60

Most gold medals
Men: 14: Michael Phelps (USA), Swimming 2004–08
Women: 9: Larysa Latynina (USSR), Gymnastics, 1956–64

Most medals in individual events
Men: 12: Nikolai Andrianov (USSR), Gymnastics, 1972–80
Women: 14: Larysa Latynina (USSR), Gymnastics, 1956–64

Youngest medal winners in an individual event
Men: 14 years 11 days: Nils Skoglund (Den), High Diving, 1920
Women: 12 years 24 days: Inge Sorensen (Den), 200m Breaststroke, 1936

Youngest gold medal winners
Men: 13 years 283 days: Klaus Zerta (Ger), Rowing, 1960
Women: 13 years 268 days: Marjorie Gestring (USA), Diving, 1936

Oldest medal winners in individual event
Men: 72 years, 280 days: Oscar Swahn (Swe) Running Deer Shooting, 1920
Women: 53 years 277 days: Queeni Newall (GB), Archery, 1908

Oldest gold medal winners
Men: 68 years 256 days: Oscar Swahn (Swe) Single-shot Deer, 1920
Women: 53 years 277 days: Queeni Newall (GB), Archery, 1908

Paris 1924

The 1924 Olympic Games in Paris were officially opened by France's President, Gaston Doumergue, on 4 May 1924 at the Stade Olympique Yves-du-Manoir. It was at these Games that the Olympic Motto, 'Citius, Altius, Fortius' (Faster, Higher, Stronger), was introduced. These Games also witnessed the inaugural tradition at the Closing Ceremony of raising three flags: those of the International Olympic Committee, the host nation and the next host nation.

Johnny Weissmuller of the USA won three Swimming gold medals, in the men's 100m Freestyle, the men's 400m Freestyle and the men's 4 x 200m Freestyle Relay, plus a bronze in the men's Water Polo. He later won two more gold medals at the 1928 Games in Amsterdam and went on to achieve stardom playing Tarzan in 12 Hollywood movies. The 1924 Games witnessed the introduction of women's Fencing, with Denmark's Ellen Osiier taking the gold medal without losing a single bout. Finland's Paavo Nurmi won five gold medals to add to the three he had won at Antwerp 1920. In total, some 1,000 journalists covered the events as the Games began to attract global attention. A total of 44 nations sent 3,089 athletes (2,954 men, 135 women) to participate in 126 events across 17 sports. The Closing Ceremony took place on 27 July 1924.

Final medals table (top ten)

Pos.	Nation	Gold	Silver	Bronze	Total
1	USA	45	27	27	99
2	Finland	14	13	10	37
3	France	13	15	10	38
4	Great Britain	9	13	12	34
5	Italy	8	3	5	16
6	Switzerland	7	8	10	25
7	Norway	5	2	3	10
8	Sweden	4	13	12	29
9	Netherlands	4	1	5	10
10	Belgium	3	7	3	13

Triple generation medal winners

Andreas Keller won a gold medal with the Unified Germany team in field Hockey at Barcelona 1992 to become the third generation of his family to win a medal in the event: his grandfather, Erwin, won a silver medal at Berlin 1936; and his father, Carsten, a gold medal, again on home soil, at Munich 1972.

Inaugural medals

At the 1896 Games in Athens, event winners were awarded a silver medal, an olive branch and a diploma. Athletes who finished second were presented with a copper medal, a branch of laurel and a diploma. On the front of the medal the face of Zeus, the Greek god, was depicted along with his hand holding a globe with the winged victory on it and the caption 'Olympia', written in Greek. The back of each medal had the Acropolis site with the words 'International Olympic Games in Athens in 1896', also written in Greek.

London spawns the IAAF

The 1908 Games in London prompted the establishment of standard rules for sports, as well as the selection of judges from different countries, instead of only the host nation, to officiate at the Games. The controversial men's 400m Final also resulted in the formation of the International Amateur Athletics Federation, the purpose of which was to set uniform worldwide rules for athletics.

Daley's double gold

At Los Angeles 1984 in the men's Decathlon competition, Daley Thompson of Great Britain found himself up against his long-time rival, West Germany's Jurgen Hingsen. The two super-fit athletes were neck and neck after seven of the ten events, but Thompson went into a higher gear and pulled away from Hingsen with superb performances in the pole vault and javelin throw to all but retain his Olympic Games title. Thompson then set his sights on breaking Hingsen's world record score of 8,832 points. The champion at Moscow 1980 needed to run the final event, the 1500m, in a time of no more than 4:34.58 to break Hingsen's world record, but he clocked 4:35.00, appearing to ease up as he approached the finishing line. Thompson's gold medal score was given as 8,798 points, while Hingsen claimed the silver with 8,673 points – West Germany's Siegfried Wentz took bronze with 8,412 points. The following year, however, IAAF officials re-examined the photo timer results at the 1984 Games and found that Thompson had clocked a time of 14.33 seconds in the 110m Hurdles, as opposed to the 14.34 seconds he was originally given, making his overall score 8,847 points – a new world record. The engaging, if occasionally controversial, Thompson won the BBC Sports Personality of the Year Award in 1982 and was awarded the OBE in 1983, followed by a CBE in 2000.

Paavo Nurmi (1897–1973)

1 Paavo Johannes Nurmi was born on 3 June 1897 in Turku, Finland.

2 At the age of 12, he became a vegetarian and did not eat meat for the rest of his life.

3 A champion at every distance from 1500m to 10,000m, he was the second athlete (after Hannes Kolehmainen) to be known as the 'Flying Finn'.

4 Nurmi competed at three Olympic Games: Antwerp 1920, Paris 1924 and Amsterdam 1928.

5 He won a record total of nine gold medals and three silver in Athletics at the Olympic Games.

6 At Antwerp 1920, Nurmi won gold in the men's 10,000m and both Team and Individual Cross-Country.

7 He won five gold medals at Paris 1924, retaining his two Cross-Country titles and winning the men's 1500m, men's 5000m and men's 3000m Team events.

8 At Amsterdam 1928, he won the men's 10,000m and was second in the men's 5000m and the men's 3000m Steeplechase.

9 Just before the 1932 Olympic Games in Los Angeles, he was branded a professional and could not run in the men's Marathon, an event he claimed he would have 'won by five minutes'.

10 Nurmi lit the Olympic Flame at the Opening Ceremony for the 1952 Olympic Games in Helsinki.

11 On 2 October 1973, Paavo Nurmi died in Helsinki and was given a state funeral.

12 A statue of Paavo Nurmi was sculpted and stands outside Helsinki's Olympic Stadium.

Did you know that?

There is a 13,000-capacity sports stadium in Turku named in Paavo Nurmi's memory. It stages athletics meetings and football matches.

Olympics go orbital

A 115-metre tall spiralling structure, named the ArcelorMittal Orbit, designed by the Turner Prize-winning artist Anish Kapoor has been chosen as the monument that will be placed within the Olympic Park at the London 2012 Games. Kapoor's masterpiece, which will cost £19.1 million, incorporates the five Olympic Rings. At 22m taller than New York's Statue of Liberty, it will offer visitors far-reaching views of London.

Olympic Games talk (7)

'Success in sport as in almost anything comes from devotion. The athlete must make a devotion of his specialty.'
Hudson Strode's *description of Paavo Nurmi*

Drug tests introduced

Knud Jenson, a Danish cyclist, died as a result of a drug overdose during the men's Road Race at Rome 1960. His death shocked the IOC and cycling's governing body, the International Cycling Federation, which became the first international body to introduce drug tests.

The first football World Cup

At the 1928 Games in Amsterdam, Uruguay retained its Football title, beating South American rivals Argentina 1–0 in a replay after the first match ended 1–1. Both nations had reached the final with relative ease. Uruguay beat the host nation, the Netherlands, 2–0 in the round of the last 16 and followed this with a 4–1 win over Germany in the quarter-finals and a 3–2 victory over Italy in the semi-finals. Argentina hammered the USA 11–2 in the round of 16, beat Belgium 6–3 in the quarter-finals and thrashed Egypt 6–0 in their semi-final. The attractiveness of an all-South American final created enormous interest, and not just with the football-mad Dutch public, as 250,000 requests for tickets came in from all over Europe. Uruguay's Hector Scarone scored the winning goal in the replay of the final, while Uruguay's double-gold achievement was recognised the following year when the FIFA Congress, held in Barcelona, awarded the Uruguayans the honour of playing host to the inaugural FIFA World Cup finals in 1930. Uruguay were crowned FIFA World Cup champions on 30 July 1930 after defeating Argentina 4–2 in the final played in Montevideo. Up to 1928, the Football tournament at the Games was regarded as football's world championship. In fact, the Football tournaments at Antwerp 1920 (with 14 participating nations), Paris 1924 (22) and Amsterdam 1928 (17) all had a greater number of participants than the first World Cup, in 1930, which had 13.

Greek triumph

Fencer Leonidas Pyrgos became Greece's first champion of the modern Games by winning the men's masters Foil competition at Athens 1896.

McDonald's at the Olympic Games

In the lead-up to the 1984 Games in Los Angeles, the McDonald's fast food giant ran a promotion in which every customer buying a Meal Deal received a scratch-card. Each card revealed an Olympic Games event, with the promise that if the USA won a gold medal in the event the customer would win a free item from their menu. When the Soviet Union led a 14-nation boycott of the Games, withdrawing two months before they were held, McDonald's reportedly lost millions of dollars, as the USA won 83 gold medals. This incident was parodied in a 1992 episode of the hit cartoon television series *The Simpsons* ('Lisa's First Word'), in which Krusty the Clown decided to run a promotion in his fast food store, and the Krusty Burger was named as the 'Official Meat-Flavored Sandwich of the 1984 Olympics'. The same principle applied, with scratch-cards being handed out with the promise that if the USA won the event then the customer would win a free Krusty Burger. But Krusty tried to rig the competition by putting on the scratch-cards only those events usually dominated by Eastern bloc countries. When the Games were boycotted, Krusty lost US$44 million.

Bird's Nest hosts the world

The track and field events at the 2008 Olympic Games were held in Beijing National Stadium – known as 'The Bird's Nest', because of its highly distinctive twig-like structural elements and bowl-shaped roof. It seated 100,000 spectators for the Games but its capacity was later reduced to 80,000. Built on Beijing's Olympic Green, it was designed by the Pritzker Prize-winning Swiss architects Jacques Herzog and Pierre de Meuron – designers of London's Tate Modern gallery – while Chinese contemporary artist Ai Weiwei was the artistic consultant. The stadium cost 3.5 billion Chinese yuan (£215 million) to build.

Fulfilling high expectations

Dutch cyclist Leontien van Moorsel lived up to the huge billing she was given in the lead-up to the 2000 Games in Sydney by winning three gold medals and one silver medal. She won the women's Road Race, the women's Time Trial and the women's Individual Pursuit and claimed a silver medal in the women's Points race. At Athens 2004, she retained her women's Time Trial crown and won a bronze medal in the women's Individual Pursuit. During her career, van Moorsel also won four track World Championships gold medals and four road World Championships gold medals.

Pakistan end Indian rule

In the men's Hockey competition during the 1960 Games in Rome, Pakistan prevented their bitter rivals, India, from claiming a seventh consecutive gold medal in the event. India had won the previous six men's Hockey titles at the Games, dating back to Amsterdam 1928, but had to settle for silver in Rome, with Spain winning the bronze. It was also the first ever Olympic Games gold medal won by Pakistan.

Gold medal in three classes

Soviet sailor Valentyn Mankin won the gold medal in the Finn class at Mexico City 1968. Four years later, at Munich 1972, he entered the Tempest class and won gold with Vitaly Dyrdyra. At Montreal 1976, he claimed a silver medal in the Tempest class alongside a new partner, Vladyslav Akimenko. When the 1980 Games were held in Moscow, in his native Russia, the 41-year-old Mankin teamed up with Aleksandrs Muzichenko and entered the Star class. Remarkably, they claimed the gold medal in the final race, making Mankin the only sailor in history to win gold medals in three different classes at the Games.

Who's the granddaddy?

At the 1908 Games in London, Sweden's shooter Oscar Swahn won two gold medals in the Single-shot Running Deer Individual and Team events. He also won a bronze medal in the Double-shot Running Deer Individual event. Swahn was 60 years old, a year younger than Britain's Joshua Kearney 'Jerry' Miller, who claimed gold in the Individual Free Rifle at 1,000 yards. Miller was 61 years and four days old when he won his gold medal. At Stockholm 1912, on home soil, Swahn was again a member of the Single-shot Running Deer Team that won the gold medal. He also secured a second successive bronze medal in the Individual Double-shot Running Deer event. At 64 years old he became the oldest ever gold medallist at the Games, a record that still stands. Finally, aged 72, he was the oldest competitor at the Antwerp 1920 Games, where he managed a fourth-place finish in the Team Single-shot Running Deer event and a silver medal in the Team Double-shot Running Deer competition. His silver medal made him the oldest medallist of any colour of all time (excluding the art competitions) at the Games – 72 years and 279 days old. Illness prevented the 76-year-old Swahn from participating in the 1924 Games in Paris and he died on 1 May 1927.

Amsterdam 1928

The 1928 Olympic Games in Amsterdam were officially opened on 17 May 1928 by His Royal Highness Prince Hendrik. Amsterdam had made unsuccessful bids to host the Games in 1920 and 1924. At the Opening Ceremony, the Greek athletes led the Parade of Nations, with the host nation, the Netherlands, marching into the Olympisch Stadion last. Thus a new protocol was established: Greece first, hosts last. Henri Denis, a Dutch footballer, pronounced the Olympic Oath. Amsterdam 1928 saw the number of female athletes more than double after the IOC finally permitted them to enter Gymnastics and Athletics.

The 1928 Games saw Asian competitors winning gold medals for the first time: Japan's Mikio Oda won the men's Triple Jump (Asia's first Olympic champion in an individual event), and his compatriot, Yoshiyuki Tsuruta, won the men's 200m Breaststroke in the Swimming competition. In the men's Hockey tournament, India claimed the gold medal to begin a dominance of the sport at the Games, winning the first of six consecutive gold medals. Hungary, however, began an even more impressive streak by claiming the first of seven consecutive gold medals in men's Team Sabre Fencing. A total of 46 nations sent 2,883 athletes (2,606 men, 277 women) to participate in 109 events across 14 sports. The Closing Ceremony took place on 28 August 1928.

Final medals table (top ten)

Pos.	Nation	Gold	Silver	Bronze	Total
1	USA	22	18	16	56
2	Germany	10	7	14	31
3	Finland	8	8	9	25
4	Sweden	7	6	12	25
5	Italy	7	5	7	19
6	Switzerland	7	4	4	15
7	France	6	10	5	21
8	Netherlands	6	9	4	19
9	Hungary	4	5	0	9
10	Canada	4	4	7	15

IOC calls for a truce

At Barcelona 1992, for the first time in Olympic Games history, the International Olympic Committee launched an appeal for the observance of the Olympic Truce.

Comaneci claims triple gold

Nadia Comaneci, born on 12 November 1961 in Onesti, Romania, and the winner of five gold medals in Gymnastics at the Games, took up the sport at the age of six after the Romanian coach Bela Karolyi noticed her and a friend turning cartwheels in a schoolyard. At the 1976 Games in Montreal, 14-year-old Comaneci won three gold medals (in the Individual All-Around Competition, Balance Beam and Uneven Bars), a silver (in the Team Competition) and a bronze (in the Floor). She was the first Romanian gymnast to win the Olympic Games All-Around title and she holds the record as the youngest ever All-Around Gymnastics champion. This latter record will never be broken, because gymnasts must now be at least 16 years of age in the calendar year to compete at the Olympic Games. At Moscow 1980, Nadia successfully defended her title on the Balance Beam and tied with Nellie Kim (USSR) for the gold medal in the Floor competition, her fifth gold medal at the Games. Also at Moscow 1980, she won silver medals in the All-Around and Team Competitions.

The most famous losing Olympian

Dorando Pietri was first to cross the finishing line in the men's Marathon at the 1908 Games in London. Sadly, however, he was disqualified after the race because officials had helped the dazed and confused Italian to finish. Indeed, ten minutes of his 'winning' time of 2:54:46 seconds were required to assist him over the final 350 metres of the race. As Pietri told the *Corriere della Sera* newspaper on 30 July 1908, 'I am not the Marathon winner. Instead, as the English say, I am the one who won and lost victory.'

One leg, six medals

The USA's George Eyser won six medals at St Louis 1904: three gold (25-foot Rope Climbing, Long Horse Vault and Parallel Bars), two silver (4-events All-Around and Pommel Horse) and a bronze (Horizontal Bar). He won all his medals despite having a wooden leg. Eyser's left leg had been amputated after he had been run over by a train.

Fallen runner

Portugal's Francisco Lazaro collapsed from dehydration during the men's Marathon at Stockholm 1912. Tragically, he died the next day at the Serafimer Hospital of heat exhaustion.

The Big Kahuna

Duke Paoa Kahinu Mokoe Hulikohola Kahanamoku, nicknamed 'The Big Kahuna', won the gold medal in the men's 100m Freestyle Swimming event at Stockholm 1912. The 1916 Games were cancelled because of the First World War, but at Antwerp 1920 he retained his men's 100m Freestyle title. Kahanamoku had participated in an amateur swimming event in Honolulu Harbor on 11 August 1911, and swam the 100m Freestyle in a time of 55.4 seconds, beating the existing world record by 4.6 seconds. When his time was sent to Amateur Athletic Union officials in New York, the AAU replied: 'Unacceptable. No one swims this fast. Hawaiian judges alerted to use stop watches, not alarm clocks!'

Down Under on top

During the 1956 Games in Melbourne, Australian swimmers cleaned up in the pool. They won all of the men's and women's Freestyle races and claimed a total of 14 medals (eight gold, four silver and two bronze) from the 13 Swimming events in one of the most dominant team displays ever witnessed at a single Games. The USA team were the next most successful with 11 medals. In both the men's and women's 100m Freestyle events, Australian swimmers occupied the first three places and the hosts also won both Relay races. Two Australians doubled up: Murray Rose became the first male swimmer to win two Freestyle events (400m and 1500m) since Johnny Weissmuller in 1924; and Dawn Fraser won gold medals in the women's 100m Freestyle and was the lead-off swimmer in Australia's successful 4 x 100m Relay team.

Speed machine

Great Britain's Chris Boardman won the men's 4000m Individual Pursuit Track gold medal at Barcelona 1992, riding a revolutionary new 'super bike'. Four years later, at Atlanta 1996, he elected not to defend his title but opted for the 52-kilometre Time Trial, where he won a bronze medal. Boardman became so famous after Barcelona 1992 that he was regularly mentioned on television. During an episode of the popular comedy *Only Fools and Horses*, Del Boy, played by David Jason, is at his pitch in the market attempting to sell some dodgy cycling helmets. At one point he shouts to the passing shoppers: 'Cycling helmets, as worn by Chris Boardman, and by his brother Stan Boardman [an unrelated stand-up comedian].'

Olympic Games talk (8)

'As long as Morceli (Noureddine Morceli) is in the race, it is always a race for second place.'
Venuste Niyongabo, *Burundi athlete at Atlanta 1996*

Modern Summer Olympic Games hosts

Year	Host City/Nation	Year	Host City/Nation
1896	Athens, Greece	1964	Tokyo, Japan
1900	Paris, France	1968	Mexico City, Mexico
1904	St Louis, USA	1972	Munich, West Germany
1908	London, England	1976	Montreal, Canada
1912	Stockholm, Sweden	1980	Moscow, USSR
1920	Antwerp, Belgium	1984	Los Angeles, USA
1924	Paris, France	1988	Seoul, South Korea
1928	Amsterdam, Holland	1992	Barcelona, Spain
1932	Los Angeles, USA	1996	Atlanta, USA
1936	Berlin, Germany	2000	Sydney, Australia
1948	London, England	2004	Athens, Greece
1952	Helsinki, Finland	2008	Beijing, China
1956	Melbourne, Australia	2012	London, England
1960	Rome, Italy	2016	Rio de Janeiro, Brazil

The original 'Flying Finn'

Finland's Juho Pietari ('Hannes') Kolehmainen, who won three gold medals at Stockholm 1912, was the first of many great long-distance runners to be dubbed "The Flying Finn". He won the men's 5000m in a world record time of 14:36.06 and set a world record in the men's 3000m in a heat of the Team event. He also won a silver medal in the Cross-Country Team event. Finland's athletes dominated at Stockholm 1912, winning four other track gold medals. However, at the time, Finland was ruled by Russia, and although the country sent a team to the Games, when a Finnish athlete won a gold medal, it was the Russian flag that was raised during the Victory Ceremony, leading Kolehmainen to say that he almost wished he hadn't won. At the first post-World War One Games, at Antwerp 1920, Kolehmainen won another gold medal, this time in the men's Marathon. In the intervening years, Hannes and his brother, Willie, spent time in the USA (Hannes finished fourth in the 1917 Boston Marathon) training under the guidance of an American coach, and when the brothers returned home, they helped train other Finnish athletes.

Olympic Flag at half-mast

On the second day of the 2000 Games in Sydney the President of the IOC, Juan Antonio Samaranch, had to return home as his wife was severely ill. However, by the time he got there she had already died. Samaranch returned to Sydney four days later and the Olympic Flag was flown at half-mast as a mark of respect. Canada's flag also flew at half-mast in the Olympic Village following the death of their former Prime Minister, Pierre Trudeau.

Eight days, seven golds

Over a period of eight days at the 1972 Games in Munich, Mark Spitz (USA) entered seven Swimming events, won them all and set a new world record in every final. Spitz's medal feat was surpassed at Beijing 2008, when Michael Phelps won eight gold medals which, combined with his six from Athens 2004, makes him the most successful competitor in the history of the Olympic Games.

Second World War games

The 1940 Olympic Games, the Games of the XII Olympiad, were first awarded to Tokyo, Japan. By mid-1938, however, Japan was at war with China and withdrew. The IOC then awarded the Games to Helsinki, Finland, but they also withdrew after the 1939 invasion by the Soviet Union. With the world at war, the Games were then cancelled, as were those in 1944, when London was due to be the Host City.

A living legend

At the Opening Ceremony of the 1996 Games in Atlanta, one of the oldest living sportsmen was in attendance, 97-year-old gymnast Leon Stukelj from Yugoslavia. In Paris 1924, he won the men's Horizontal Bars and men's All-Around gold medals. At Amsterdam 1928, he won gold on the Rings plus two bronze medals (in the men's All-Around and in the Team competition). He missed Los Angeles 1932, like many other athletes who could not afford the cost of crossing the Atlantic. Finally, at Berlin 1936, he won a silver medal on the Rings, at the age of 37. At Atlanta 1996 he shook hands with US President Bill Clinton and was afforded the honour of presenting the medals to winners in the men's Team Gymnastics competition, much to the delight of spectators and gymnasts alike. Stukelj died on 12 November 1999, just four days short of his 101st birthday.

Tarzan ends Japanese rule

At Los Angeles 1932, Japanese swimmers claimed gold in every men's Swimming event except for the 400m Freestyle, which was won by Larry 'Buster' Crabbe from the USA. He, like Johnny Weissmuller before him, went on to play Tarzan. Crabbe made his debut in a 1933 television serial, *Tarzan the Fearless*, and starred in more than 100 movies. Americans dominated in the women's Swimming events, claiming four of the five gold medals. Helene Madison won gold in the women's 100m and 400m Freestyle races and a third gold as a member of the 4 x 100m Freestyle Relay team.

The first all-round Olympian

Eric Lemming was born in Gothenburg, Sweden, on 22 February 1880, and at the age of 19 he set a world record of 49.31 metres in the javelin. The following year, Lemming travelled to compete in the 1900 Games in Paris. However, as the javelin was not an Olympic discipline, the young Swede participated in six other events. He finished fourth in the men's High Jump, men's Pole Vault and men's Hammer, and eighth in the men's Discus Throw. At the 1906 Intercalated Games in Athens, Lemming competed in nine different events. He won the men's Freestyle Javelin Throw gold medal, setting a new world record, and won bronze medals in the men's Pentathlon, men's Shot Put and the men's Tug of War, and finished fourth in the men's Discus and the men's Stone Throw. At London 1908, while Lemming was still the world record holder, the Javelin Throw was accepted as a full-medal event. Lemming won the men's Freestyle Javelin (the event was dropped after London 1908) and broke his own world record to claim gold in the regular men's Javelin Throw with a throw of 54.825m. He also finished eighth in the men's Hammer and participated in the men's Discus Throw and men's Greek-style Discus Throw. At Stockholm 1912, aged 32, Lemming made a final appearance at the Games, held in his home country. He won the gold medal in the men's Javelin Throw with a new world record in excess of 60m, the first athlete to exceed the mark. The appreciative crowd gave their hero a much-deserved standing ovation. Lemming also took fourth place in a one-time event in which the competitors threw the Javelin with each hand. During his career, Lemming set ten javelin world records, including his swan-song, a post-1912 Olympic Games throw of 62.32m. He died in Gothenburg aged 50 on 5 June 1930. His half-brother, Oscar Lemming, competed at London 1908 and Stockholm 1912, but did not win a medal.

Los Angeles 1932

The 1932 Olympic Games in Los Angeles were officially opened on 30 July 1932 by Charles Curtis, Vice-President of the USA. The Opening Ceremony took place in the superb Los Angeles Olympic Stadium (later renamed the Los Angeles Memorial Coliseum), where the Olympic Oath was given by George Calnan (Fencing). Los Angeles had been the only city to offer to host the Games, as the world was still suffering from the effects of the Great Depression, which had begun in 1929. Indeed, because of the high cost of travelling to the USA, the Games managed to attract just over half the number of participants from four years earlier (at Amsterdam 1928). However, despite the relatively small number of athletes – 1,332 (1,206 men and 126 women) – the level of competition was very high, with 18 world records either broken or equalled at the Games (16 of them in men's track and field events). The American public welcomed the Games to their country, with record crowds in attendance, including 100,000 at the Opening Ceremony.

Among the firsts witnessed at the 1932 Games were electronic timing to 1/100th of a second, the use of the photo-finish camera, the three-tier victory podium, the playing of national anthems and the raising of national flags at the medal ceremonies.

The star of the Games was 21-year-old American Mildred Didrikson, who qualified for all five women's track and field events. However, 'Babe', as she was affectionately nicknamed, was allowed to compete in only three of the events: she won the women's Javelin Throw and set world records in the women's High Jump and the women's 80m Hurdles to claim three gold medals. A total of 37 nations sent their athletes to participate in 117 events across 14 sports. The Closing Ceremony took place on 14 August 1920.

Final medals table (top ten)

Pos.	Nation	Gold	Silver	Bronze	Total
1	USA	41	32	30	103
2	Italy	12	12	12	36
3	France	10	5	4	19
4	Sweden	9	5	9	23
5	Japan	7	7	4	18
6	Hungary	6	4	5	15
7	Finland	5	8	12	25
8	Great Britain	4	7	5	16
9	Germany	3	12	5	20
10	Australia	3	1	1	5

16-year-old gold medallist

Ulrike Meyfarth of West Germany won the gold medal in the women's High Jump at the 1972 Games in Munich. She beat her personal best by 7 centimetres to equal the world record (1.92 metres) and, aged 16 years and 114 days, become the youngest person of either sex to win an Athletics Olympic Games gold medal in an individual event. After Munich 1972 her career went on a bit of a rollercoaster. She failed to qualify for the women's High Jump Final at Montreal 1976, did not compete when West Germany boycotted the 1980 Games in Moscow, but claimed her second gold medal in the women's High Jump at Los Angeles 1984. This time she became the oldest female to win the women's High Jump title at the Games.

Dutch public sponsor the Games

In May 1925, the Dutch Olympic Committee published an appeal in which they asked the general public for help with raising funds to host the 1928 Olympic Games in Amsterdam. Within two weeks the generous Dutch public had donated more than 1.5 million guilders.

15-minute miler in the pool

At the 1980 Games in Moscow, Vladimir Salinkov (USSR) won three Swimming gold medals (the men's 400m Freestyle, the men's 1500m Freestyle and the men's 4 x 200m Freestyle Relay). In the final of the men's 1500m Freestyle, he won the gold medal in a time of 14:58.27, becoming the first swimmer in history to break the magic 15-minute barrier (considered to be the equivalent of breaking the four-minute barrier for the mile on the track). Salinkov missed the 1984 Olympic Games in Los Angeles on account of the Soviet boycott, but he won the gold medal in the men's 1500m Freestyle again at Seoul 1988.

Out of the black into the red

The official budget of the organising committee for London 1908 was £15,000. More than £5,000 of the budget was put aside for 'entertainment expenses', while most of the revenue for the Games did not come from ticket sales (which accounted for 28 per cent of revenue) but from donations. With receipts for the Games totalling £21,377, the organisers claimed a profit. However, they failed to include the construction of the White City Stadium, which cost the British tax-payer £60,000.

Olympic Games talk (9)

'I can only say that working with Big John was one of the highlights of my life. He was a Star (with a capital "S") and he gave off a special light and some of that light got into me. Knowing and being with Johnny Weissmuller during my formative years had a lasting influence on my life.'

Actor **Johnny Sheffield**, who played 'Boy' in the Tarzan movies alongside Johnny Weissmuller

A podium of one

During the men's 400m final at London 1908, a major incident occurred that later resulted in a change of the rules at future Olympic Games. Great Britain's Wyndham Halswelle reached the Final after setting the fastest qualifying time, a new Games record of 48.4 seconds. In the final, Halswelle lined up against three American runners, John C. Carpenter, William Robbins and John Taylor. As the four athletes came into the final stretch of the race, Robbins was leading, followed by Carpenter, with Halswelle third. Carpenter and Halswelle then both swung out to pass Robbins when a race official, Roscoe Badger, shouted 'Foul!' Carpenter crossed the line in first place followed home by Robbins, with Halswelle third. However, the British race officials accused Carpenter of blocking Halswelle and voided the race. Although photographic evidence showed that Carpenter did block Halswelle, under US athletics rules blocking in a race was permitted. Unfortunately for Carpenter, the race was run under the stricter British rules, so the officials ordered a re-run, this time in lanes, and without Carpenter, whom they disqualified. When Robbins and Taylor decided not to run, out of loyalty to their team-mate Carpenter, Halswelle ran the race alone and won the gold medal. It remains the only occasion in Olympic Games history in which the final of an event has been a walk-over. As a direct result of the controversy surrounding the race, since Stockholm 1912 all 400m races have been run in lanes.

East Germany's golden girl

Kristin Otto was the dominant force in the pool at the 1988 Games in Seoul, winning six gold medals (in the women's 50m Freestyle, 100m Butterfly, 100m Freestyle, 100m Backstroke, 4x100m Freestyle and 4 x 100m Medley Relay). She was named Female World Swimmer of the Year in 1984, 1986 and 1988 by *Swimming World* magazine.

Women's 200m fantasy Olympic Games Final

Lane No./Athlete	Country	Olympic Medals
1 Irena Szewinska	Poland	Gold – Mexico City 1968, Silver – Tokyo 1964
2 Fanny Blankers-Koen	Netherlands	Gold – London 1948
3 Marie-José Pérec	France	Gold – Atlanta 1996
4 Renate Stecher	E. Germany	Gold – Munich 1972, Bronze – Montreal 1976
5 Valerie Brisco-Hooks	USA	Gold – Los Angeles 1984
6 Bärbel Wöckel	E. Germany	2 Gold – Montreal 1976 and Moscow 1980
7 Veronica Campbell	Jamaica	2 Gold – Athens 2004 and Beijing 2008*
8 Gwen Torrence	USA	Gold – Barcelona 1992

* = Campbell (lane 7) won in 2008 under her married name (Campbell-Brown)

Johnny Weissmuller (1904 – 84)

1 Johann Peter (Johnny) Weissmuller was born in Freidorf, Austria-Hungary (now Romania) on 2 June 1904.

2 The Weissmuller family sailed to America in 1905, where his father Peter Weissmuller worked as a brewer.

3 He dropped out of high school and did a variety of jobs, including being a lifeguard.

4 Working as a lift operator and bellboy at the Illinois Athletic Club, he was spotted by swimming coach William Bachrach, who became his trainer.

5 In August 1921, he won the US national championship at 50 yards and 220 yards and, a year later, broke the world 100m record.

6 At the 1924 Games in Paris, he won three gold medals, in the men's 100m, men's 400m and men's 4 x 200m Freestyle Relay, all in the Freestyle discipline.

7 Four years later, at Amsterdam 1928, Weissmuller repeated his men's 100m and men's 4 x 200m Freestyle Relay successes.

8 As an amateur, he won 52 US national championships events, broke 67 world records and allegedly never lost a race.

9 After retiring from sport, Weissmuller became a movie star, most famously as Tarzan in a series of films, but also as Jungle Jim.

10 He appears in the collage on the front of The Beatles' *Sgt Pepper's Lonely Hearts Club Band* album.

11 Johnny Weissmuller died at the age of 79 on 20 January 1984, in Acapulco, Mexico, where he had moved with his fifth wife, Maria, four years earlier.

12 At his funeral, as his coffin was being lowered into the ground, his famous Tarzan call was played three times.

Did you know that?

In addition to his Swimming gold medals at Paris 1924, Johnny Weissmuller also won a bronze medal as a member of the USA Water Polo team.

Australia expects

One of 11 Indigenous Australians in the team of 628 at the 2000 Games in Sydney, Cathy Freeman was chosen to light the Olympic Flame. Having won women's 400m gold at the 1997 and 1999 World Championships, an expectant nation hoped she would win the event at the Games. She did not disappoint and a nation celebrated.

Argentina halt dominant USA

In the men's Basketball tournament at Athens 2004, Argentina prevented the USA from winning their fourth consecutive gold medal by defeating them 89–81 in the semi-finals. Argentina went on to beat Italy 84–69 in the final to claim the gold medal, while the USA had to settle for bronze. In the women's tournament, the USA won their third consecutive title, while Australia claimed the silver and Russia the bronze.

Professionals play at the Games

At Los Angeles 1984, for the first time in Olympic Games history, professional footballers were permitted to compete in the Football tournament. The only condition was that they must not have played in a FIFA World Cup finals tournament. France defeated Brazil 2–0 in the final in front of 101,799 spectators at the Rose Bowl, Pasadena. Yugoslavia overcame Italy 2–1 to win the bronze medal.

A case of two Germanys

At the 1952 Olympic Games in Helsinki, the two Germanys were invited back after a 16-year absence since the 1936 Games in Berlin. West Germany entered under the aegis of a new National Olympic Committee (NOC), the Federal Republic of Germany (FRG). East Germany also established a new NOC after the Second World War, the German Democratic Republic (GDR), but did not send any athletes to Helsinki.

Vive La France

France's Marie-Jose Perec won the women's 200m at Atlanta 1996 and broke the 400m Games record to claim a second gold medal. She had won the women's 400m gold at Barcelona 1992 and during her career collected two European Championship gold medals and one bronze, plus two golds in the IAAF World Championships. She is the most successful French female athlete of all time and the first female athlete to make a successful defence of the women's 400m title at the Games. However, just before the start of the 2000 Games in Sydney, Perec left the Olympic Village in a cloud of controversy and withdrew from the women's 400m, where she should have raced against home favourite Cathy Freeman, who went on to win gold. Perec had been harassed by the Australian press from the moment she arrived in Sydney.

Berlin 1936

The Opening Ceremony of the 1936 Games in Berlin was held in the purpose-built Olympic Stadium on 1 August 1936 and the Games were officially opened by the German Chancellor Adolf Hitler. The National Socialist (Nazi) party's propaganda machine attempted to showcase the Games to the world as Hitler's vision of a new Germany, but his plan to prove his theories of Aryan racial superiority backfired on him – at least in the Athletics events. The hosts won a total of only five gold medals in track and field – only one more than the black US athlete Jesse Owens achieved on his own.

Owens was the major star of the Games, winning gold in the men's 100m, the men's 200m, the men's 4 x 100m Relay and the men's Long Jump. German weightlifter Rudolf Ismayr gave the athletes' Olympic Oath and the Olympic Flame was lit by the athlete Fritz Schilgen. Only one other city had put in a bid to host the 1936 Games, Barcelona, but Berlin's bid was preferred by the IOC in April 1931, which was before the Nazi party came to power in Germany. A total of 49 nations sent 3,963 athletes (3,632 men, 331 women) to participate in 129 events across 19 sports at the Games. The Closing Ceremony took place on 16 August 1936.

Final medals table (top ten)

Pos.	Nation	Gold	Silver	Bronze	Total
1	Germany	33	26	30	89
2	USA	24	20	12	56
3	Hungary	10	1	5	16
4	Italy	8	9	5	22
5	Finland	7	6	6	19
	France	7	6	6	19
7	Sweden	6	5	9	20
8	Japan	6	4	8	18
9	Netherlands	6	4	7	17
10	Great Britain	4	7	3	14

Bitten but not beaten

The most controversial gold medal at Paris 1924 was unquestionably that of Great Britain's Harry Mallin in the Middle Weight division of the Boxing competition. Frenchman Roger Brousse was initially declared the winner following his bout with Mallin, but a Swedish official complained that the Briton had been bitten by his opponent during the fight and Brousse was subsequently disqualified.

Keep your medals, we don't want 'em

The USA's men's Basketball team first lost a match in the Games at Munich 1972. They went into the Final against the USSR with an unblemished 62–0 record dating back to 1936. With just three seconds of the game left on the clock, the USSR led 49–48 before committing a hard foul on Doug Collins, who made two free throws to put the USA 50–49 in front. The Brazilian referee, Renaldo Righetto, blew his whistle to restart play with a single second of the game remaining. However, the USSR's coach, Vladimir Kondrashkin, called for a time-out in between Collins's free throws – although the rules of the game clearly state that a coach cannot call a time-out during free throws. The USA intercepted the inbound pass and began to celebrate victory on the court. However, the General Secretary of FIBA, R. William Jones of Great Britain, permitted the time-out and ordered that three seconds be placed on the game clock. When the Russians inbounded the ball, Alexander Belov scored a lay-up to claim a dramatic 51–50 victory. The USA team refused to accept the silver medal during the Victory Ceremony and lodged an appeal. However, this was rejected in a 3–2 vote by the five-judge appeal panel made up of judges from Cuba (against), Hungary (against), Italy (for), Poland (against) and Puerto Rico (for). The Basketball Final at Munich 1972 is widely considered to be the most dramatic and exciting team contest ever witnessed at an Olympic Games.

Modern Pentathlon first

Women took part in the Modern Pentathlon for the first time in Olympic Games history at Sydney 2000, and it was joy for Great Britain as Stephanie Cook won the gold medal. The USA's Emily de Riel took the silver, and Britain's Kate Allenby the bronze. Cook was a rower at Cambridge and only took up the modern pentathlon while completing her clinical medicine course at Oxford.

Nine Olympic Games

Austrian sailor Hubert Raudaschl became the first person ever to compete in nine Olympic Games when he competed at Atlanta 1996. His consecutive Games appearances began at Tokyo 1964, and it was nearly ten Olympic Games in a row as he had been a reserve at the 1960 Games in Rome. Raudaschl won two silver medals, one in the Finn class at Mexico City 1968 and the other in in the Star class at Moscow 1980.

The Pocket Hercules

Naim Suleymanoglu was born in Ptichar, Bulgaria, but represented Turkey in weightlifting. In 1986, during a trip to the Weightlifting World Cup finals in Melbourne, Australia, he defected and ended up in Turkey, where he successfully applied for citizenship. He won three gold medals at the Games (at Seoul 1988, Barcelona 1992 and Atlanta 1996) in the Featherweight division (56–60 kilograms), seven World Championships and six European Championships. He also broke world records a staggering 46 times. Standing just 4 foot 11 inches tall, he was nicknamed the 'Pocket Hercules'. At Sydney 2000, he missed out on a fourth consecutive gold medal when he had failed to lift 145kg (a weight that would have broken the Games record). In 2001 Suleymanoglu was awarded the Olympic Order, the highest accolade of the Olympic Movement.

Unusual sports of 1900

Some quite unusual sporting events were contested for the first and only time at the 1900 Games in Paris. These included the Equestrian High Jump and Equestrian Long Jump, Live Pigeon Shooting, a Swimming Obstacle Race and Underwater Swimming. The Obstacle Race required both swimming underneath and climbing over rows of boats. In the Underwater Swimming event, France's Charles de Venville won gold after staying submerged for more than one minute. Meanwhile, the Belgian athlete, Leon Lunden, shot 21 birds on his way to the Live Pigeon Shooting gold medal.

Romans end pagan games

After Greece became part of the Roman Empire in 146 BC, the Olympic Games, which had begun in 776 BC, continued for several centuries. But after the Christianisation of Rome, the Games came to be viewed as a pagan festival and in contravention of Christian values. In AD 393, the Emperor Theodosius I banned the Games, bringing an end to a tradition that had lasted more than 1,000 years.

Red Army officer

Vladimir Petrovich Kuts was serving as an officer in the Russian Army when he went to the 1956 Games in Melbourne as a long-distance runner. He won the men's 10,000m final easily and five days later claimed a second gold when he won the men's 5000m.

War hero and great Olympian

At the 1908 Games in London, Georges Yvan ('Geo') Andre, born in Paris on 13 August 1889, made his Olympic Games debut in the men's High Jump. Prior to arriving in England, the 18-year-old's best jump had been 1.79 metres, but he cleared 1.88m and won the silver medal. Four years later, at Stockholm, Andre entered the men's 110m Hurdles, men's Decathlon, men's High Jump, men's Pentathlon, men's Standing High Jump and men's Standing Long Jump, but didn't win a medal. During the First World War he fought as a soldier, was seriously injured and then captured and imprisoned by the Germans. After making numerous attempts to escape he finally succeeded and rejoined the French forces as a fighter pilot and won a military medal. At the 1920 Games in Antwerp he won a bronze medal in the men's 4 x 400m Relay. At Paris 1924, in the city of his birth, he took the Olympic Oath on behalf of all the athletes. Aged 34 years, and participating in his fourth Games, he repeated his Antwerp 1920 result in the men's 400m Hurdles with a fourth-place finish. In total, he competed in 13 different disciplines spanning four Olympic Games. Andre died on 4 May 1943.

Olympic Games talk (10)

'The Olympic Games are always a special competition. It is very difficult to predict what will happen.'
Sergei Bubka, *Soviet Union pole vaulter, Seoul 1988 Games*

And let the Games begin

At the inaugural meeting of the International Olympic Committee (IOC) held in the Sorbonne, Paris, in 1894, Baron Pierre de Coubertin proposed that the Olympic Games should be revived and that the first modern Games should be held in Paris in 1900 to coincide with the Universal Exhibition or World's Fair planned for the city in 1900. The delegates from the ten other countries represented at the Congress did not want to wait six years to revive the Games, and some proposed London as a venue for the first modern Games, to be held in 1896. De Coubertin, however, was against London staging the event and so he proposed Athens, the original home of the Olympic Games, and the other delegates unanimously agreed with this second suggestion. In other business at the Congress, the Greek delegate Demetrius Vikelas was elected as the IOC's first President.

Lightbody cleans up

The USA's Jim Lightbody won three gold medals at St Louis 1904: the men's 2500m Steeplechase, the men's 800m and, finally, the men's 1500m, in which he set a new world record on his way to gold. Later on the same day that won the men's 1500m final, Lightbody also won a silver medal in the men's Four-Mile Team event with his Chicago Athletic Association team-mates. At the 1906 Intercalated Games at Athens, he again won the gold medal in the men's 1500m and took silver in the men's 800m to bring his Olympic Games total to six medals. However, during the early part of the 20th century, the IOC downgraded the 1906 Games, resulting in the non-recognition by the IOC of the two medals he won in Athens.

Raincoat for a gold medal

The women's 4 x 400m Relay Final at London 1948 was held on the final day of the track and field competitions. The Dutch team had qualified for the final, but with the race drawing near it was discovered that their sprint star, Fanny Blankers-Koen, who had already won three gold medals at the Games (in the women's 100m, women's 200m and women's 80m Hurdles), was missing. She had gone shopping for a raincoat, but returned to Wembley Stadium in time to anchor the Dutch team to victory over the Australians.

Did you know that?
On 7 August 1955, Fanny won her final event, the women's shot put in the Dutch championships. It was her 58th Dutch title.

Water babies

Hungary's Deszo Gyarmati is the greatest water polo player in the sport's history. Gyarmati won five medals at five successive Olympic Games (golds at Helsinki 1952, Melbourne 1956 and Tokyo 1964; silver at London 1948; and bronze at Rome 1960) and captained Hungary to victory in the 1954 and 1962 European Water Polo Championships. After his playing career ended, he coached the Hungarian team to Water Polo gold at Montreal 1976. Gyarmati married Eva Szekely, winner of the women's 200m Breaststroke gold medal at Helsinki 1952, and their daughter Andrea won a silver medal at Munich 1972, in the women's 100m Backstroke. Andrea Gyarmati married Mihaly Hesz, Hungary's Canoeing champion at Mexico City 1968.

Olympism

'Olympism' is a state of mind based on equality of sports that are international and democratic. Furthermore, it is a philosophy of life, whereby athletes utilise the qualities of their body, their determination and their mind to 'go faster, further and higher'.

No world records

No world records were set at Athens 1896, mainly because few of the world's top athletes had travelled to Greece to take part. The USA's Thomas Burke won both the men's 100m and the men's 400m in times of 12.0 seconds and 54.2 seconds respectively.

Boycott benefactors

At Moscow 1980, the Italian and French teams benefited from the US-led boycott: Italy won eight gold medals, four times as many as they had done at Montreal 1976, while France claimed six golds in Moscow, compared to two in Montreal. The 1980 Games were also the most successful since Melbourne 1956 for a number of other nations, including Great Britain and Ireland, who competed under the British Olympic Association flag, while Bulgaria and Spain won their first-ever medals in men's track events. In total, athletes from 25 different countries won gold, and athletes from 36 different countries took home a medal.

Show me the money

At the 1928 Games in Amsterdam, spectators could purchase souvenirs depicting the five Olympic Rings for the first time. The commercialisation of the Games had begun.

'Barcelona'

The main musical theme of the 1992 Olympic Games was a song entitled 'Barcelona', written in 1987 by Freddie Mercury, the lead singer of Queen. Freddie was to have sung the song as a duet with Montserrat Caballe, the Spanish operatic soprano, during the Opening Ceremony. However, because of Mercury's untimely death on 24 November 1991, the song was used instead to accompany a film celebrating the city that was shown at the beginning of the Opening Ceremony.

London 1948

The 1948 Olympic Games in London were the second to be staged in the British capital. Because of the Second World War, the Games of the XII and XIII Olympiads had been cancelled. The Opening Ceremony took place in Wembley Stadium on 29 July 1948 and the Games were officially opened by HRH King George VI. In the women's Individual Foil Fencing, Hungary's Ilona Elek retained her crown, while Czech Jan Brzak won a second successive gold medal in the Canadian Pairs 1000m. US athlete Bob Mathias, aged only 17, won gold in the men's Decathlon just two months after graduating from high school and only four months after taking up the sport. He remains the youngest male athlete in history to win a track and field event at the Games. Fanny Blankers-Koen, a 30-year-old mother of two from the Netherlands, went into the Games as the world record holder in six events (women's 80m hurdles, women's 100m, women's 200m, women's 4 x 100m relay, women's high jump and women's long jump) but she was only permitted to compete in four under Games rules at the time. She dropped the High Jump and the Long Jump and won gold in each of the other four. John Mark (Athletics) lit the Olympic Flame, and his team-mate Donald Finlay (Athletics) gave the Olympic Oath. A total of 59 nations sent 4,104 athletes (3,714 men, 390 women) to participate in 136 events across 17 sports at the Games. The Closing Ceremony took place on 14 August 1948.

Final medals table (top ten)

Pos.	Nation	Gold	Silver	Bronze	Total
1	USA	38	27	19	84
2	Sweden	16	11	17	44
3	France	10	6	13	29
4	Hungary	10	5	12	27
5	Italy	8	11	8	27
6	Finland	8	7	5	20
7	Turkey	6	4	2	12
8	Czechoslovakia	6	2	3	11
9	Switzerland	5	10	5	20
10	Denmark	5	7	8	20

Seven-Games woman

Kerstin Palm, a Swedish fencer, became the first woman to take part in seven Olympic Games when she competed at Seoul 1988. Her best finish was fifth in the women's Individual Foil at Mexico City 1968.

The Friendship Games

The Soviet-led boycott of the 1984 Games in Los Angeles resulted in athletes from 14 nations staying at home. However, those 14 nations had won a staggering 51 per cent of the medals (and 58 per cent of the golds) at Montreal 1976. The boycotting nations now organised the 'Friendship Games' (Druzhba-84), which were held in nine different countries between July and September 1984 and included 24 sports on the Olympic Games programme. The athletes' winning time in 28 of the 41 track events at the Friendship Games was faster than that of the Los Angeles 1984 gold medallist. For example: Evelyn Ashford of the USA ran 10.97 seconds to win the women's 100m gold medal at Los Angeles, whereas East Germany's Marlies Gohr won the Friendship Games final in 10.95. Twenty-one world records were set at Los Angeles 1984, whereas 48 were set at Druzhba-84 (of which 22 were by athletes from the USSR).

On your blocks

At London 1948, starting blocks were introduced for the first time and used in races from the 100m to the 400m.

The General's diary

Among the competitors at the 1912 Games in Stockholm was the American George S. Patton, the future Second World War General. He entered the men's Modern Pentathlon and finished fifth.

Flying in thin air

The USA's Bob Beamon shattered the world record in the men's Long Jump at Mexico City 1968 with an enormous first leap of 8.90 metres (29 feet 2½ inches), beating the existing world record mark by almost two feet. Whereas the altitude (7,349 feet above sea level) affected a number of the athletes, it appeared to help Beamon glide over the sand pit beneath him. Beamon's jump was so long that the judges had to use a metal tape measure after the optical measuring device slid off its rail.

No more cinders

Tokyo 1964 was the last time a cinder running track was used for women's individual Athletics events at an Olympic Games.

Olympic Games talk (11)

'When we stage the Games it will inspire kids all over the country. A kid in Scotland or Ireland will be encouraged to take up sport.'
Daley Thompson, *double Decathlon gold-medal winner at the Games, on the fillip London 2012 will give to young athletes*

Truly inspirational words

The last line from Alfred Lord Tennyson's 1833 poem 'Ulysses' has been chosen to provide inspiration for the athletes attending the London 2012 Games. The line 'To strive, to seek, to find, and not to yield' will adorn a wall in the Olympic Village. A panel of experts chose the line after nominations were requested from the public as part of the Winning Words initiative for the Cultural Olympiad. When the players walk out on to the Centre Court at Wimbledon for the Tennis competition, they will pass under a quote from Rudyard Kipling's 'If' – 'If you can meet with triumph and disaster and treat those two impostors just the same'.

Gold for Lennox Lewis

Lennox Lewis, representing Canada, won the Super Heavy Weight (+91kg) Boxing gold medal at Seoul 1988, beating Riddick Bowe in the final. Both fighters went on to become the world Heavy Weight boxing champion during their professional careers.

'The Sparrow From Minsk'

Russian gymnast Olga Korbut won six Olympic Games medals, four gold and two silver. She burst on to the world scene at Munich 1972, where her warm smile and captivating performances melted the hearts of the audience at a time when the Cold War was still being played out. At Munich, 'The Sparrow from Minsk' won gold in the Team Competition, Balance Beam and Floor. On the Beam in Munich, she became the first gymnast ever to do a backward somersault (a move that has since become known as the 'Korbut Flip') and was also the first gymnast to do a standing backward somersault on the Uneven Bars, the event at which she won a silver medal at Munich. Four years later, at Montreal 1976, where Romania's Nadia Comaneci was the star of the Games (winning three gold medals), Korbut claimed her fourth gold medal and won silver medals in the Team Competition and on the Balance Beam.

Trying to make a splash

Held at the port of Kiel, Water Skiing was one of the demonstration sports at the 1972 Olympic Games in Munich. A total of 35 competitors representing 20 nations took to the water, with the unofficial gold medals awarded across three disciplines – Slalom, Figure Skating and Jumping – for both men and women.

First African Olympians

Among the men's Marathon runners at St Louis 1904 were Len Tau and Jan Mashiani, a pair of Tswana tribesmen. They were in St Louis as part of the Boer War Exhibition at the World's Fair and became the first Africans to compete at the Games. Tau finished ninth and Mashiani finished 12th, but Tau might have won the race if he had not been chased nearly a mile off course by a large, aggressive dog.

Asterix at the Olympic Games

The live-action movie *Asterix and Obelix at the Olympic Games* was released in the run-up to Beijing 2008. In this Olympic Games story, the Gauls, on hearing that the Romans are planning to send legionary Gluteus Maximus to represent Rome at the Olympiad in Greece, decide to send their own champions, Asterix and Obelix. Unfortunately for them, the Greek officials ban the magic potion as it is an artificial stimulant, and so Asterix and Obelix must compete as mere mortals. However, Asterix manages to persuade the Romans to drink the potion, which sees them kicked out of the Games, leaving Asterix the winner of the 'Golden Palm'. The famous French actor, Gérard Depardieu, played the role of Obelix for the third time.

Did you know that?
When Paris was bidding to host the 1992 Games, their bid committee published a poster depicting Asterix holding a torch over the Eiffel Tower, while a brief *Asterix at the Olympics* story was also written to promote the bid. The IOC chose Barcelona as the Host City.

Least populated medal winners

At the 1976 Games in Montreal, Bermuda, with a mere 53,500 inhabitants, became the least populated country to win a medal at an Olympic Games when boxer Clarence Hill won the bronze medal in the Heavy Weight division.

More than an Athletics stadium

The following stadia that have played host to an Olympic Games have also hosted other major sporting events:

Athens – Olympiako Stadio
1983 European Cup final, 1994 and 2007 UEFA Champions League finals, 1997 IAAF World Championships, 2007 WRC Acropolis Rally SuperSpecial Stage 2005 and 2006 2006 IAAF World Cup

Beijing – Bird's Nest Stadium
2015 Athletics World Championships (scheduled)

Berlin – Olympiastadion
2006 FIFA World Cup final

Helsinki – Olympiastadion
1983 and 2005 IAAF World Championships

London – Wembley Stadium (original)
1966 FIFA World Cup final, 1996 UEFA European Championship final, five UEFA European Cup finals 1963–92

London – White City Stadium
1934 Empire Games

Los Angeles – Memorial Coliseum
Super Bowl I (1967), Super Bowl VII (1973), 1959 World Series

Melbourne – Melbourne Cricket Ground
1992 Cricket World Cup final, 2006 Commonwealth Games, annual Australian Football League Grand final

Moscow – Grand Arena of the Central Lenin Stadium (now Luzhniki)
2007 UEFA Champions League final, 2013 IAAF World Championships (scheduled)

Munich – Olympiastadion
1974 FIFA World Cup final, 1979 European Cup final, 1988 UEFA European Championship final, 1993 and 1997 UEFA Champions League finals

Paris – Stade Olympique de Colombes
1938 FIFA World Cup final

Rome – Stadio Olimpico
1977 and 1984 European Cup finals, 1987 IAAF World Championships, 1990 FIFA World Cup final, 1996 and 2009 UEFA Champions League finals

Sydney – Stadium Australia (now Telstra Stadium)
2003 RWC Rugby World Cup final, annual National Rugby League Grand final

Tokyo – National Olympic Stadium
1991 IAAF World Championships

Men's 400m fantasy Olympic Games Final

Lane No./Athlete	Country	Medals
1 Alberto Juantorena	Cuba	Gold – Montreal 1976
2 Eric Liddell	GB	Gold – Paris 1924
3 Michael Johnson	USA	2 Gold – Atlanta 1996 and Sydney 2000
4 George Rhoden	Jamaica	Gold – Helsinki 1952
5 Viktor Markin	USSR	Gold – Moscow 1980
6 Jeremy Wariner	USA	Gold – Athens 2004, Silver – Beijing 2008
7 Lee Evans	USA	Gold – Mexico City 1968
8 Steve Lewis	USA	Gold – Seoul 1988, Silver – Barcelona 1992

Helsinki 1952

The 1952 Olympic Games in Helsinki were officially opened by President Juho Kusti Paasikivi on 19 July 1952 at the Olympic Stadium. However, prior to President Paasikivi's official opening speech the spectators watched as Paavo Nurmi, Finland's nine-time Olympic Games champion (1920, 1924 and 1928), entered the stadium with the Olympic Flame. The 55-year-old Nurmi lit a cauldron on the ground, and young football players then carried the Torch up to the top of the stadium tower, where another former Finnish Olympic Games champion, Hannes Kolehmainen (who won four Athletics gold medals in 1912 and 1920), lit the Olympic Cauldron. Heikki Savolainen (Gymnastics) gave the Olympic Oath. Both Nurmi and Kolehmainen, middle- and long-distance running champions, would have been impressed with the exploits of Emil Zatopek (Czechoslovakia) at Helsinki 1952. He became the only person in Olympic Games history to win the men's 5000m, the men's 10,000m and the men's Marathon at the same Games. Helsinki 1952 witnessed the first ever participation by the Soviet Union (Russia had competed at the Stockholm 1912 Games) although they insisted that their athletes live in a separate Olympic Village. Indeed, the Soviet women's Gymnastics team impressed everyone with their athleticism by winning the Team Competition very comfortably, thereby beginning a winning streak that would last until the Soviet Union broke up into separate republics. Israel also made their inaugural appearance at the Games, while women were permitted to compete against men in the Equestrian Dressage event for the first time. A total of 69 nations sent 4,955 athletes (4,436 men, 519 women) to participate in 149 events across 17 sports. The Closing Ceremony took place on 3 August 1952.

Final medals table (top ten)

Pos.	Nation	Gold	Silver	Bronze	Total
1	USA	40	19	17	76
2	USSR	22	30	19	71
3	Hungary	16	10	16	42
4	Sweden	12	13	10	35
5	Italy	8	9	4	21
6	Czechoslovakia	7	3	3	13
7	France	6	6	6	18
8	Finland	6	3	13	22
9	Australia	6	2	3	11
10	Norway	3	2	0	5

Olympic Torch reignited

The Olympic Cauldron at the Los Angeles Memorial Coliseum was built specially for the 1932 Olympic Games (it was used again in 1984 when the Games returned to the city). In fact, the Cauldron is still lit on a regular basis. It is seen most often during the fourth quarter of USC (University of Southern California) American Football games. In addition, the Cauldron is lit to mark other special occasions: in 2004, after former US President Ronald Reagan died, it was ignited for a week as a mark of respect; in April 2005, following the death of Pope John Paul II – who had celebrated a mass at the stadium on his 1987 visit – the Cauldron was ignited once more; and it also had been lit for around ten days following the 9/11 terror attacks on the USA in 2001.

Chariots of Fire

At the 1924 Games in Paris, two British runners, Harold Abrahams and Eric Liddell, won gold medals in the men's 100m and the men's 400m respectively. Their achievements were documented in Hugh Hudson's 1981 Academy Award-winning film *Chariots of Fire*. In one important detail, however, the film is not historically accurate. Liddell, a devout Christian, knew many months in advance that the preliminary heats for the men's 100m (his favoured event) would take place on a Sunday and so, contrary to the story in the film, he had plenty of time to alter his training and prepare for the men's 400m.

20th-century master of disaster

During the 1960 Games in Rome, 18-year-old Cassius Marcellus Clay, later known as Muhammad Ali, won a gold medal in Boxing's Light Heavy Weight division, defeating his Polish opponent Zbigniew Pietryskowsky in the Final. Ali would go on to become the undisputed Heavy Weight boxing champion of the world and one of the greatest sporting icons of the 20th century.

Above all others

At London 1908, Ray Ewry from the USA won the men's Standing High Jump and men's Standing Long Jump for the third consecutive Games. Ewry is the only athlete in Olympic Games history to win a career total of eight gold medals in individual events.

Babe Zaharias (1911–56)

1. Mildred Ella 'Babe' Didrikson was born on 26 June 1911 in Port Arthur, Texas.

2. As well as excelling at a variety of sports, she was an excellent seamstress and won the 1931 South Texas State Fair sewing championship.

3. Didrikson was also a singer and harmonica player; she released a number of records.

4. At the 1932 American Amateur Athletic Union championships, she set world records in the women's 80m Hurdles, women's Javelin Throw and women's High Jump.

5. Didrikson won gold medals at the 1932 Olympic Games in Los Angeles in both the women's 80m Hurdles and women's Javelin throw and won a silver medal in the women's High Jump.

6. She won All-American awards as a basketball player, but women's Basketball was not on the Olympic Games programme until Montreal 1976.

7. She claimed that her nickname 'Babe' was in honour of Babe Ruth, the baseball player, and she excelled at baseball, softball, bowling, diving and roller-skating.

8. In 1938, Mildred married wrestler George Zaharias, who was known as 'the Crying Greek from Cripple Creek'.

9. As Babe Zaharias, she became one of the greatest of all women golfers.

10. She won ten women's majors, 41 tour events, was elected to World Golf Hall of Fame in 1954 and was a five-time Associated Press Female Athlete of the Year.

11. Zaharias was diagnosed with cancer in 1953 and won a golf major a month after undergoing surgery in 1954, but died from the disease on 27 September 1956.

12. The Babe Zaharias Museum and Babe Zaharias Park are in her hometown of Beaumont, Texas.

Did you know that?

Babe Zaharias's medal for the women's High Jump was actually half gold and half silver, the only such medal in Olympic Games history.

Deyna strikes twice

Poland won the Football gold medal at the 1972 Games in Munich when they beat Hungary 2–1 in the Final thanks to two goals from Kazimierz Deyna, who was playing for Legia Warsaw at the time.

Olympic Games talk (12)

'The greatest memory for me of the 1984 Games was not the individual honours, but standing on the podium with my team-mates to receive our Team gold medal.'

Mitch Gaylord, *American gymnast, 1984 Games in Los Angeles*

Bond, James Bond

Toshiyuki 'Harold' Sakata was born on 1 July 1920 in Holualoa, Hawaii, of Japanese descent. At the 1948 Games in London, he won a silver medal for the USA in the Heavyweight Weightlifting division, lifting a total of 410 kilograms. However, he became more famous for his role as Oddjob, the villain in the James Bond film *Goldfinger*.

Super Daley

Daley Thompson won the first of his two men's Decathlon gold medals at the 1980 Games in Moscow. He also struck gold at the IAAF World Championships (once), European Championships (twice) and at the Commonwealth Games (three times), all in the men's Decathlon. Daley's athletic success during the 1980s led to his name being used for three officially licensed home computer games manufactured by Ocean Software: *Daley Thompson's Decathlon*, *Daley Thompson's Supertest* and *Daley Thompson's Olympic Challenge*.

The golden girls

Great Britain's Ann Packer won a gold medal in the women's 800m at the 1964 Games in Tokyo. Packer had gone to Japan with her sights set on winning a gold medal in her favoured event, the women's 400m, but in that she finished second to Australia's Betty Cuthbert. With her heart set on coming home with a gold medal, Packer entered the women's 800m, a distance she had run competitively only five times previously. In her first-round heat she finished fifth and a third place in the semi-final secured a place in the final, albeit with the slowest qualifying time of the eight athletes in the field. In the final, Packer started slowly and was trailing in sixth place after 400 metres, moved up to third after 600m and then, using her 400m finishing speed, she took the lead in the final straight and raced to victory. It would take four decades for another British athlete, Kelly Holmes, to win the women's 800m gold medal at the Games, at Athens 2004.

The endurance Olympic Games

During the 1912 Games in Stockholm, the course for the Cycling Road Race stretched over 199 miles (320 kilometres), making it the longest race of any kind in Olympic Games history and the riders set off on their marathon race at 2.00am. In the men's Greco-Roman Wrestling competition, the Middleweight semi-final between the Estonian (competing for Russia) Martin Klein and Finland's Alfred Asikainen lasted 11 hours and 40 minutes. Klein won, but he was too exhausted to wrestle in the final the following day, so the gold medal went to Sweden's Claes Johanson. Finland's Hannes Kolehmainen won three gold medals in long-distance running: the men's 5000m, the men's 10,000m and the Individual Cross-Country. However, the most popular athlete at Stockholm 1912 was undoubtedly the USA's Jim Thorpe who won the men's Pentathlon and then went on to shatter the world record in the men's Decathlon.

Helsinki hero

During the 1948 Games in London, Emil Zatopek won the men's 10,000m in commanding style. On lap ten of 25 at Wembley, he moved out in front and went on to lap all but two of his rivals. He finished a full 300 metres (48 seconds) clear of his nearest rival, France's Alain Mimoun. Three days later, the Czechoslovakian ran in the final of the men's 5000m. His efforts in the men's 10,000m appeared to be taking their toll when going into the final lap he trailed the leader, Belgium's Gaston Reiff, by 50m, but Zatopek kicked into gear and almost pipped the Belgian on the line, but could manage only a silver medal, finishing just 1.5m behind Reiff. At the 1952 Games in Helsinki, Zatopek retained his men's 10,000m title and claimed a third gold medal by winning the men's 5000m. Zatopek then decided to enter the men's Marathon, although he had never run one before, and won it by two and a half minutes from Reinaldo Gorno of Argentina, much to the appreciation of the Finnish spectators, who sang his name. Zatopek thus became the only runner ever to win the men's long-distance treble of 5000m, 10,000m and Marathon at a single Games. At the 1956 Games in Melbourne, he was due to run in the men's Marathon but suffered a hernia just six weeks before the Games got under way. He ran anyway and finished in sixth place.

Did you know that?
On the afternoon of Zatopek's men's 5000m triumph at Helsinki 1952, his wife Dana won a gold medal in the women's Javelin Throw.

Royal prerogative

HRH Princess Anne, a member of Great Britain's Equestrian team, was the only female competitor at the 1976 Olympic Games in Montreal who was not required to undergo a gender test.

USA men rule

In the track and field events at Melbourne 1956, the USA men obliterated all before them, winning gold medals in 15 of the 24 events. The team achieved a 1-2-3 in four of them (the men's 200m, 110m Hurdles, 400m Hurdles and Discus), and finished first and second in five others (the men's 100m, Pole Vault, Long Jump, Shot Put and Decathlon). The American women, however, claimed just two medals from the nine events: Mildred McDaniel won the gold in the women's High Jump and the 4 x 100m Relay team took the bronze. World records were also thin on the ground in the field events, with only two being achieved. McDaniel claimed one of them with a leap of 1.76 metres (5 feet 9¼ inches). Norway's Egil Danielsen set the other in the men's Javelin with a throw of 85.71m (281 feet 2½ inches).

Hitler watches students win gold

The USA's Eights Rowing team, all members of the University of Washington, won the gold medal at the 1936 Games in Berlin by defeating Italy (silver) and Germany (bronze) as Hitler looked on.

Men's Marathon winner almost dies

Thomas J. Hicks, a brass worker from Cambridge, Massachusetts, won the men's Marathon at the St Louis 1904 Olympic Games in a time of 3:28:53. However, Hicks's win is clouded in controversy as he walked part of the route and was assisted along the way by substances which are now deemed illegal. When Hicks was struggling in the St Louis heat, his assistants dosed him with 1/60th of a grain (approximately 1 milligram) of strychnine sulphate (now banned by the IOC) and a raw egg white. The first dose of strychnine did not revive him for long, however, and he was given a second dose along with some brandy. The drugs proved too much for his body to take and he had to be helped across the finish line before collapsing. Had Hicks not received medical attention after the race ended he might well have died and the day after he won his gold medal he announced his retirement from the sport.

Melbourne 1956

The 1956 Olympic Games in Melbourne were officially opened on 22 November 1956 by HRH the Duke of Edinburgh at the Melbourne Cricket Ground. Ron Clarke lit the Olympic Flame, while John Landy gave the Olympic Oath at the first Games to be held in the southern hemisphere. The Games witnessed some outstanding achievements: Hungary's Laszlo Papp became the first boxer to win three successive gold medals when he won the Light Middle Weight event to add to the Light Middle Weight gold he won at Helsinki 1952 and the Middle Weight gold he won at London 1948. In Gymnastics, two athletes dominated: Viktor Chukarin (USSR) won five medals, including three golds (in the men's Parallel Bars, Team Competition and All-Around Individual), bringing his career total to 11 medals (seven of which were gold); and Hungary's Agnes Keleti won four gold medals (in the women's Team Portable Apparatus, Uneven Bars, Balance Beam and Floor competitions) and two silver to bring her career tally to ten medals (five gold, three silver, two bronze). The Equestrian events were held in Stockholm, Sweden, in June 1956, as Australian quarantine laws did not permit the entry of foreign horses. This was the first time that a Games was held in two countries. A total of 72 nations sent 3,314 athletes (2,038 men, 376 women) to participate in 145 events across 17 sports. The Closing Ceremony took place on 8 December 1956.

Final medals table (top ten)

Pos.	Nation	Gold	Silver	Bronze	Total
1	USSR	37	29	32	98
2	USA	32	25	17	74
3	Australia	13	8	14	35
4	Hungary	9	10	7	26
5	Italy	8	8	9	25
6	Sweden	8	5	6	19
7	United Germany	6	13	7	26
8	Great Britain	6	7	11	24
9	Romania	5	3	5	13
10	Japan	4	10	5	19

The Olympic Games' rocket man

During the Opening Ceremony at Los Angeles 1984, Bill Suitor flew into the Los Angeles Coliseum powered by a jet pack (the Bell Aerosystems rocket pack). Suitor had flown into the Coliseum before, prior to American football's Super Bowl I in 1967.

Equal rights

Women's Athletics and Gymnastics events were contested for the first time at the 1928 Games in Amsterdam. Betty Robinson (USA) won the 100m, Lina Radke (Germany) won the 800m, Canada won the women's 4 x 100m Relay, Ethel Calderwood (Canada) won the High Jump and Halina Konopacka (Poland) won the Discus Throw. The Netherlands won gold in the only Gymnastics competition contested, in the All-Round Team event, with Italy claiming silver and Great Britain taking bronze. Ethel Seymour of Great Britain became the oldest gymnastic medallist, winning her bronze at the grand age of 46 years and 6 months.

The red flying machine

The USSR's Valeri Borzov was the sprint king of Munich 1972, winning the men's 100m and the men's 200m gold medals. The USA's top two sprinters, and favourites to take the gold and silver medals in the men's 100m, Eddie Hayes and Rey Robinson, won their opening rounds but missed their next heat – they were given incorrect starting times – and were disqualified. Borzov nearly suffered the same fate, but made the starting line with seconds to spare.

Israel wins first medal

Almost 20 years after the Munich Massacre, Yael Arad became the first Israeli to win a medal at the Games – silver in Judo (61 kilogram class) at Barcelona 1992. A day later, fellow judoka Oren Smadja became the first Israeli man to win a medal, a bronze (71kg class).

Conspicuous by his absence

On the second day of the 1936 Games in Berlin, Der Fuhrer, Adolf Hitler, shook hands with two of the gold medal winners from the first two days' events, a German and a Finn, and then left the stadium. At the time many sports writers inferred that Hitler left Berlin's Olympic Stadium so as to avoid having to shake hands with Cornelius Johnson, an African-American who had won the men's High Jump gold medal on that day of the Games. However, according to an official spokesman, Hitler's early departure had been pre-scheduled. Following this, IOC officials insisted that the German Chancellor should meet and greet each and every medallist or none at all. Hitler elected to miss all further medal presentations.

Olympic Games talk (13)

'All I've done is run fast. I don't see why people should make much fuss about that.'
*Dutch athlete, **Fanny Blankers-Koen**, the biggest star of the 1948 Olympic Games in London*

Testing the winners

During the 1968 Games in Mexico City, in addition to the regular random drugs test, all gold medal winners were required to undergo a drug test. Now all the medal winners are routinely tested.

The Olympic Games' superman

Jesse Owens's greatest achievement came in a span of 45 minutes on 25 May 1935 at a track and field meeting in Ann Arbor, Michigan, USA. During the 1935 National Collegiate Athletic Association (NCAA) Championships, Owens set three world records and tied a fourth. His first world record came in the men's long jump, with a distance of 8.13 metres (26 feet 8¼ inches – a mark that would stand for 25 years); he then broke the men's 200m (220 yards) world record with a time of 20.3 seconds; in the men's 200m (220 yards) low hurdles he broke the tape in a time of 22.6 (becoming the first man to break 23 seconds); and he tied the world record for the men's 91m (100 yards) dash in a time of 9.4. Such was the enormity of Owens's achievement that, in 2005, NBC sports commentator Bob Costas and University of Central Florida Professor of Sports History Richard C. Crepeau chose this as the most impressive athletic achievement since 1850. In 1936, Owens repeated his four gold medals haul at the NCAA Championships.

Did you know that?
Prior to his world record-breaking long jump leap, Owens placed a handkerchief 26 feet 2½ inches (8.5m) beyond the takeoff board, the distance of the existing world record, as a marker. He then jumped almost six inches past it.

El Guerrouj follows in Nurmi's path

At the 2004 Olympic Games in Athens, Morocco's Hicham El Guerrouj became the first runner since Finland's Paavo Nurmi at Paris 1924 to win gold medals in both the men's 1500m and the men's 5000m.

A wet Big Mac

The Swimming events at Los Angeles 1984 were held in the McDonald's Olympic Swim Stadium. Meanwhile, the official snack product of the Games was the Snickers bar (then known as Marathon in the UK).

Racists banned

South Africa's competitors and teams were banned from the Games after Rome 1960 until Barcelona 1992. The IOC refused to endorse the racist (Apartheid) policy of the South African government.

Canadian takes on the USA

Canada's Percy Williams was the surprise winner of both the men's 100m and men's 200m at the 1928 Olympic Games in Amsterdam. Two years later, Williams won the men's 100m at the inaugural British Empire Games (Commonwealth Games) held in Hamilton, Ontario. Williams's double success at Amsterdam 1928 infuriated the Americans so much that they organised a series of indoor track meets and invited Williams to race against the best the USA had to offer. Rubbing salt into an already gaping wound, Williams won 19 of the 21 races in the series, indisputably establishing himself as the world's best sprinter at the time. Unfortunately for Williams, however, a thigh muscle injury seriously hampered his running and at the 1932 Games in Los Angeles he made it only as far as the quarter-finals. He retired from athletics and became an insurance agent.

East Germany 23, USSR 22

The East German men's Handball team beat the USSR 23–22 in the 1980 Olympic Games Final to claim their first medal of any colour in men's Handball.

First female champion at the Games

The first female champion of the modern Olympic Games was British tennis player Charlotte Cooper, who won the women's Singles at the 1900 Games in Paris. She defeated home favourite Helene Provost 6–1, 6–4 in the final. Cooper also won gold in the Mixed Doubles. Prior to the 1900 Games, Cooper had won three Wimbledon ladies' singles championships (in 1895, 1896 and 1898) and went on to capture two more (in 1901 and 1908).

For demonstration purposes only

Demonstration sports were part of the Games from 1912 to 1992. Medals were awarded, but they did not count in the official tables.

Stockholm 1912........Baseball (men)
                             Glima (martial art) (men)
Antwerp 1920..........Korfball (men)
Paris 1924...............Pelota (men)
                             La canne (French martial art) (men)
                             Canadian Canoeing and Kayaking (men)
                             Savate (French Kickboxing) (men)
Amsterdam 1928.....Kaatsen (Dutch Handball) (men)
                             Korfball (men) Lacrosse (men)
Los Angeles 1932....American Football (men)
                             Lacrosse (men)
Berlin 1936...............Baseball (men)
                             Gliding (men)
London 1948.............Lacrosse (men)
                             Swedish Ling Gymnastics (men/women)
Helsinki 1952............Finnish Baseball (men)
                             Field Handball (men)
Melbourne 1956.......Australian Rules Football (men)
                             Baseball (men)
Rome 1960................None
Tokyo 1964...............Baseball (men)
                             Budo (Japanese martial art) (men)
Mexico City 1968....Pelota (men)
                             Tennis (men/women)
Munich 1972.............Badminton (men/women)
                             Water Skiing (men/women)
Montreal 1976..........None
Moscow 1980...........None
Los Angeles 1984....Baseball (men)
                             Tennis (men/women)
Seoul 1988................Badminton (men/women)
                             Baseball (men)
                             Bowling (men/women)
                             Judo (women)
                             Taekwondo (men/women)
Barcelona 1992........Pelota (men/women)
                             Roller Hockey (men)
                             Taekwondo (men/women)

Life before glory

At the first modern Olympic Games, in Athens in 1896, Hungary's Alfred Hajos won both the men's 100m Freestyle and the men's 1200m Freestyle Swimming events. Both races were held on the same day, 11 April, and for the 1200m race the contestants were transported by boat and left to swim back to shore alone. After his 1200m victory Hajos remarked: 'I must say that I shivered at the thought of what would happen if I got a cramp from the cold water. My will to live completely overcame my desire to win.'

Princess Anne

At Montreal 1976, Princess Anne competed for Great Britain in the Equestrian event. The winner of the 1971 European three-day event championship, she once said: 'The horse is about the only person who does not know you are Royal.'

The Dream Team

Legendary basketball player Michael Jordan won two gold medals at the Games. He was part of the USA's team at Los Angeles 1984, when he was still at college, and at Barcelona 1992 he was a member of the 'Dream Team'. The star-studded team, which included fellow NBA legends Larry Bird, Magic Johnson, Charles Barkley, Patrick Ewing, Chris Mullin, Scottie Pippen and David Robinson, won all eight of their games in Barcelona, scoring an average of 117 points and did not take a single time-out during the competition.

Did you know that?
Jordan, Ewing and Mullin are the only American players to win gold medals for men's Basketball at the Games as college players, or amateurs (in 1984), and as NBA professionals (1992).

Nadia the Cat

In the American television series *Lost*, the character Mikhail Bakunin – played by Andrew Divoff – named his cat Nadia after the multiple gold-medal winner Nadia Comaneci. Bakunin referred to her as 'the greatest athlete the world has ever known' and claimed he shared a birthday with the Romanian star. Comaneci was the first gymnast to successfully perform an aerial cartwheel, a double back handspring and an aerial walkover on the Balance Beam.

Rome 1960

The 1960 Olympic Games came to Italy (Rome) 52 years after the country had been forced to give up the hosting rights for the 1908 Games in the aftermath of the 1906 Mount Vesuvius eruption. To win the right to stage the 1960 Games, Rome beat off competition from six other candidate cities: Brussels, Budapest, Detroit, Lausanne, Mexico City and Tokyo. President Giovanni Gronchi officially opened the Games on 25 August 1960 in the Stadio Olimpico, with Giancarlo Peris (Athletics) lighting the Olympic Flame and Adolfo Consolini (Athletics) performing the Olympic Oath.

The Games witnessed some outstanding individual performances, notably Hungary's Aladar Gerevich winning his sixth consecutive gold medal in Fencing (in the Team Sabre event), Sweden's Gert Fredriksson winning his sixth gold medal in the Canoe events, and Denmark's Paul Elvstrom winning a fourth consecutive gold medal in Sailing. Boxer Clement 'Ike' Quartey of Ghana became the first black African to win a medal at the Games when he took the silver at Light Welter Weight and, five days later, Ethiopia's Abebe Bikila, who ran barefoot, won the gold medal in the men's Marathon to become the Games' first black African champion. The USA's Wilma Rudolph won three gold medals in the women's 100m, 200m and 4 x 100m Relay – remarkable given that she overcome polio when she was a child (and was the 20th of 22 children). Rudolph became the first American woman to win three Athletics gold medals at a single Games. The hosts had their own hero, Sante Gaiardoni, who became the only cyclist ever to win both the men's Time Trial and Match Sprint events. A total of 84 nations sent 5,338 athletes (4,727 men and 611 women) to participate in 150 events across 17 sports at the Games. The Closing Ceremony took place on 11 September 1960.

Final medals table (top ten)

Pos.	Nation	Gold	Silver	Bronze	Total
1	USSR	43	29	31	103
2	USA	34	21	16	71
3	Italy	13	10	13	36
4	United Germany	12	19	11	42
5	Australia	8	8	6	22
6	Turkey	7	2	0	9
7	Hungary	6	8	7	21
8	Japan	4	7	7	18
9	Poland	4	6	11	21
10	Czechoslovakia	3	2	3	8

Gold for Brasher after appeal

Great Britain's Chris Brasher was the first athlete to cross the finish line in the men's 3000m Steeplechase at Melbourne 1956. However, to Brasher's amazement, the judges disqualified him, claiming that he had interfered with Norway's Ernst Larsen and announced Hungary's Sandor Rozsnyoi as the gold-medal winner. Brasher appealed against the judges' decision and was supported in his appeal by Larsen and a few other competitors. The judges reversed their decision and Brasher became the first Briton to win an Athletics gold medal since Los Angeles 1932, when Thomas Hampson won the men's 800m and Thomas Green the men's 50km Walk.

A profitable Games

Despite being held at a time when there was a worldwide economic depression, the 1932 Games in Los Angeles made a profit for the organisers of US$1 million. The figure is even more remarkable when you take into account the fact that the Americans paid for the accommodation costs of the Games (they built the first Olympic Village), gave free food to all of the athletes and even paid for the athletes' entertainment during the 16 days of events.

Japanese hosts clean up

Two new sports first appeared at Tokyo 1964: men's Judo and Volleyball (both men's and women's). Three of the four gold medals in the Judo divisions went to the host nation, Japan: Takehide Nakatani (Lightweight), Isao Okano (Middleweight) and Isao Inokuma (Heavyweight) – Anton Geesink of the Netherlands won gold in the open category. In Volleyball, the USSR won the men's gold medal, while the women's gold went to Japan. Women's Volleyball was the first women's team sports event contested at an Olympic Games.

When winter meets summer

Before Paris 1924, it was decided, after much debate, that winter sports would be added to the Olympic Games the same year. The inaugural Olympic Winter Games were held in Chamonix, France, from 25 January to 4 February 1924. It started a tradition of the Olympic Winter Games being staged a few months before the Summer Games. Since 1994, the Winter Games have been staged in alternate even-numbered years, between the Summer Games.

Olympic Games talk (14)

'There can be distractions, but if you're isolated from the heart of the Games, the Olympics become just another competition.'
Mary Lou Retton, American gymnast, Los Angeles 1984

The master race

During the 1936 Games in Berlin, Hitler's 'master race' Germany topped the medals table, winning a total of 89 medals (33 of them gold). The USA came second with 56 medals (24 gold).

A thirsty Games

The 1928 Games in Amsterdam witnessed the first appearance of Coca-Cola as a sponsor. The giant American soft drinks manufacturer sponsored the entire American team with 1,000 crates of Coca-Cola... and they have been involved ever since.

Jesus wins triple men's Hammer Throw gold

At the 1900 Games in Paris the Irish-born John 'Jesus' Flanagan (representing the USA) won the men's Hammer Throw competition, beating fellow American Truxton Hare by 4.75 metres. At St Louis 1904, Flanagan successfully defended his title, defeating John DeWitt by less than one metre with a throw of 51.23m. Then, at the 1908 Games in London, Flanagan beat the world record holder, Matt McGrath, with his final throw to win his third consecutive men's Hammer Throw gold medal. On 24 July 1909, aged 41 years and 196 days, Flanagan recorded a throw of 56.18m to become the oldest world record holder in the history of Athletics. In 1911, he returned to his native Ireland, where he stayed until his death in 1938.

Elementary for Holmes

At the 2004 Olympic Games in Athens, Great Britain's Kelly Holmes won gold medals in both the women's 800m, in a time of 1:56.38, and the women's 1500m (in a time of 3:57.90).

When two become one

At London 1908, Australia and New Zealand were represented by a single delegation, under the name of Australasia.

Women's 400m Fantasy Olympic Games Final

Lane No./Athlete	Country	Medals
1 Tonique Williams-Darling	Bahamas	Gold – Athens 2004
2 Marie-José Perec	France	2 Gold – Barcelona 1992 and Atlanta 1996
3 Marita Koch	East Germany	Gold – Moscow 1980
4 Valerie Brisco-Hooks	USA	Gold – Los Angeles 1984
5 Cathy Freeman	Australia	Gold – Sydney 2000
6 Christine Ohuruogu	Great Britain	Gold – Beijing 2008
7 Irena Szewinska	Poland	Gold – Montreal 1976
8 Betty Cuthbert	Australia	Gold – Tokyo 1964

Dorando Pietri (1885 – 1942)

1 Dorando Pietri was born in Correggio, Italy, on 7 February 1885 and grew up in the northern town of Carpi.

2 As an 18-year-old working in a confectionery shop in Carpi, he learned of a local street race, where he took on and beat Italian champion Pericle Pagliani.

3 A few weeks later he ran in a men's 3000m race in Bologna and finished second.

4 In 1906, Pietri qualified for the men's Marathon at the Athens 1906 Intercalated Games and he was leading the race by five minutes when he was forced to retire through illness.

5 He was Italian champion in 1907, winning events from 5000m to the Marathon.

6 Training for the 1908 Games in London, he ran a 40-kilometre race in Carpi in a time of 2:38:00.

7 The men's Marathon at London 1908 started from Windsor Castle in mid-afternoon on 24 July. It was an exceptionally hot day by English standards.

8 Pietri took the lead at 39km (3.195 miles short of the finish), but collapsed near the finish and was helped over the line.

9 The US team, for whom Johnny Hayes was second, protested the result and the Italian was disqualified.

10 Queen Alexandra, under whose balcony at Windsor Castle the men's Marathon had begun, awarded Pietri a gilded silver cup as compensation.

11 He turned professional and won marathons around the world, achieving a personal best time of 2.38:48.2 in Buenos Aires.

12 Pietri died aged 56 in San Remo, Italy, from a heart attack on 7 February 1942.

Did you know that?
Irving Berlin, the famous composer, dedicated a song to Dorando Pietri entitled, simply, 'Dorando'.

Osties and Westies

At the 1976 Games in Montreal, the women's 100m and 200m events were completely dominated by German athletes. The women's 100m was won by West Germany's Annegret Richter followed by East Germany's Renate Stecher, with Richter's team-mate Inge Helten claiming bronze. East Germany's Bärbel Eckert won the women's 200m, with Richter taking silver and Stecher taking bronze.

Top medal-winning nations

Year	Olympiad	Location	NOCs	Most Medals G-S-B–Total
1896	I	Athens, GRE	14	Greece (10–19–18—47)
1900	II	Paris, FRA	26	France (26–37–32–95)
1904	III	St Louis, USA	13	USA (78–84–82—244)
1906*	—	Athens, GRE	20	France (15–9–16—40)
1908	IV	London, GBR	22	Britain (54–46–38—138)
1912	V	Stockholm, SWE	28	Sweden (23–24–17—64)
1916**	VI	Berlin, GER		
1920	VII	Antwerp, BEL	29	USA (41–27–27—95)
1924	VIII	Paris, FRA	44	USA (45–27–27—99)
1928	IX	Amsterdam, NED	46	USA (22–18–16—56)
1932	X	Los Angeles, USA	37	USA (41–32–30—103)
1936	XI	Berlin, GER	49	Germany (33–26–30—89)
1940**	XII	Tokyo, JPN (Helskinki, FIN)		
1944**	XIII	London, GBR		
1948	XIV	London, GBR	59	USA (38–27–19—84)
1952	XV	Helsinki, FIN	69	USA (40–19–17—76)
1956	XVI	Melbourne, AUS	72	USSR (37–29–32—98)
1960	XVII	Rome, ITA	83	USSR (43–29–31—103)
1964	XVIII	Tokyo, JPN	93	USSR (30–31–35—96)
1968	XIX	Mexico City, MEX	112	USA (45–28–34—107)
1972	XX	Munich, W GER	121	USSR (50–27–22—99)
1976	XXI	Montreal, CAN	92	USSR (49–41–35—125)
1980	XXII	Moscow, USSR	80	USSR (80–69–46—195)
1984	XXIII	Los Angeles, USA	140	USA (83–61–30—174)
1988	XXIV	Seoul, S KOR	159	USSR (55–31–46—132)
1992	XXV	Barcelona, SPA	169	UT*** (45–38–29—112)
1996	XXVI	Atlanta, USA	197	USA (44–32–25—101)
2000	XXVII	Sydney, AUS	199	USA (40–24–33—97)
2004	XXVIII	Athens, GRE	202	USA (35–39–29—103)
2008	XXIX	Beijing, CHN	204	USA (36–38–36—110)

*Intercalated Games ** Games cancelled due to a World War*
**** Unified Team of 12 former USSR Republics*

The greatest team ever assembled

At the 1960 Games in Rome, the greatest men's amateur Basketball team ever assembled won the gold medal. Team USA'S 12-man squad included Oscar Robertson, Jerry West, Jerry Lucas, Walt Bellamy and Terry Dischinger, four of whom would go on to win the NBA Rookie of the Year Award between 1961 and 1964.

Tokyo 1964

The 1964 Olympic Games were held in Tokyo, Japan – the first Games to be hosted by an Asian nation. The Opening Ceremony took place on 10 October 1964 and was conducted by the Emperor Hirohito. In testimony to the rebuilding of the country after the Second World War, the Olympic Flame was lit by Yoshinori Sakaï, a student who was born on 6 August 1945, the day the world's first atomic bomb exploded in Hiroshima. The Olympic Oath was performed by Takashi Ono (Gymnastics). A number of notable individual performances stood out: Dezso Gyarmati, a member of the Hungarian Water Polo team, won his fifth successive medal at the Games; Australia's Dawn Fraser won the women's 100m Freestyle Swimming gold medal for the third time; and the American swimmer Don Schollander won four gold medals. In Athletics, Ethiopia's Abebe Bikila retained his men's Marathon title – the first athlete to do so. However, the star of the games was the Soviet Union's Larysa Latynina, who won two gold, two silver and two bronze medals to bring her overall Olympic Games medal tally to an astonishing 18. A total of 94 nations sent 5,151 athletes (4,473 men, 678 women) to participate in 163 events across 19 sports.

Final medals table (top ten)

Pos.	Nation	Gold	Silver	Bronze	Total
1	USA	36	26	28	90
2	USSR	30	31	35	96
3	Japan	16	5	8	29
4	United Germany	10	22	18	50
5	Italy	10	10	7	27
6	Hungary	10	7	5	22
7	Poland	7	6	10	23
8	Australia	6	2	10	18
9	Czechoslovakia	5	6	3	14
10	Great Britain	4	12	2	18

London 2012 Games posters

In June 2011, 12 British artists were chosen to design the official London 2012 posters: Fiona Banner, Michael Craig-Martin, Martin Creed, Tracey Emin, Anthea Hamilton, Howard Hodgkin, Gary Hume, Sarah Morris, Chris Ofili, Bridget Riley, Bob and Roberta Smith and Rachel Whiteread. All the posters will be shown at a free exhibition at Tate Britain as part of the London 2012 Festival.

Munich remembered

The events of the Munich Massacre (which saw 11 Israeli team members murdered at the 1972 Olympic Games) were chronicled in the Oscar-winning documentary *One Day in September*. Later they were dramatised by Steven Spielberg in his 2005 movie *Munich*. Other films made of the Munich Massacre include *Sword of Gideon*, *21 Hours at Munich* and *Munich – Mossad's Revenge*.

A heroic hobble

Great Britain's Derek Redmond tore his hamstring in the semi-final of the men's 400m at the 1992 Olympic Games in Barcelona and fell in agony to the ground. The stretcher-bearers ran on to the running track, but Derek refused to quit. Instead, he got up and limped on in agony, but his father Jim who was watching could not bear to see his son in pain and broke through the tight security cordon to help his son. Derek completed his lap resting on his father's shoulder as 65,000 fans inside the stadium stood to their feet to applaud the brave athlete as he crossed the finishing line.

One leg, three medals

Olivier Halassy, a member of Hungary's Water Polo team, won his third Olympic Games medal at Berlin 1936. What makes his achievement even more remarkable is that he had only one leg, the other having been amputated below the knee following a streetcar accident.

Medals introduced

The 1904 Olympic Games at St Louis were the first at which gold, silver and bronze medals were awarded to the winner, runner-up and third-placed athletes in an event's final.

Shine a light

The Olympic Torch Relay for the London 2012 Games will start in Land's End, Cornwall, on 18 May 2012 and will cover 12,875 kilometres over the following 70 days before arriving in London for the Opening Ceremony of the Games on 27 July. A total of 8,000 people will carry the Olympic Torch. It will travel for 12 hours per day as it attempts to go within an hour's travel of 95% of the UK population.

Olympic Games talk (15)

'The Athens 2000 Games will be meaningful even though I cannot participate as an athlete, since I can participate in the Torch Relay all over the world.'
Cathy Freeman, *women's 400m runner, Sydney 2000 champion*

The gold medal collector

On 16 July 1900, at the Paris Games, the USA's Raymond Clarence 'Ray' Ewry won three gold medals in the standing jump events – the men's Standing High Jump, Standing Long Jump and Standing Triple Jump. Four years later, at St Louis 1904, Ewry successfully defended all three titles. Then, at London 1908, Ewry won his third gold medal in the men's Standing High Jump and Standing Long Jump (the Standing Triple Jump was discontinued after 1904). If the two gold medals Ewry won at the 1906 Intercalated Games in Athens are included, then he won a total of ten Olympic gold medals, making him the second most successful male athlete in the history of the modern Games, after swimmer Michael Phelps. Ewry's world record in the Standing Long Jump – 3.47 metres – was still standing when the event was discontinued internationally during the 1930s.

Sweden wins battle of the nations

It is quite often the case that the nation hosting the Games finishes top of the overall medals table. At the 1912 Olympic Games in Stockholm, Sweden was the most successful nation, claiming 23 gold, 24 silver and 16 bronze medals. It was the first and only time that the Swedes have finished first in the 'Battle of the Nations'.

China's top female athlete

China's Deng Yaping won four women's Table Tennis gold medals. At Barcelona 1992 she won gold in the Singles competition and partnered Hong Qiao to gold in the Doubles. Four years later, at Atlanta 1996, she retained both titles, winning a second Doubles gold with Hong Qiao. Amazingly, Deng Yaping retired when she was just 24 years old, but she left her mark on the sport, having won four Olympic Games gold medals and 18 World Championship titles. From 1990 to 1997 she was number-one ranked female player in the world and it was no surprise when she was voted Chinese Female Athlete of the Century.

Aussie golden girl of 1956

Australia's Betty Cuthbert won three gold medals for the host nation during the 1956 Olympic Games in Melbourne (in the women's 100m, 200m and 4 x 100m Relay). Today there is a statue of 'Golden Girl' Cuthbert outside the Melbourne Cricket Ground, the stadium in which she claimed her triple gold-medal haul. Eight years later, at Tokyo 1964, she won gold in the women's 400m. Bobby Joe Morrow (USA) also won three gold medals at Melbourne 1956 – in the men's 100m, 200m and 4 x 100m Relay.

Women into Construction

Given that women currently represent only 11 per cent of the construction workforce in the UK and that many of these jobs are office based (with only two per cent of women working in manual jobs in the construction industry), the 'Women into Construction' project was designed to promote construction-related employment opportunities for women. Funded by the London Development Agency and Construction Skills, it recruited and placed 266 women directly into jobs on the Olympic Park for the 2012 Games in London. In total 877 women have worked on the Olympic Park and 166 women have worked on the Athlete Village since construction started. The Women into Construction project was established in 2008 and has gone on to help women gain access training and employment opportunities on the Park with contractors across all trades including electricians, bricklayers, carpenters, traffic marshals, engineers, plumbers, dumper-truck drivers, security guards and signallers. ODA Head of Equality, Inclusion, Employment and Skills Loraine Martins said: 'We are on track and firmly focused on the finish line and it's important to recognise the contribution made by the women on site in helping deliver the Olympic Park and Village on time and within budget.'

The first Olympic Village

At the 1932 Games in Los Angeles, all the male athletes were housed in a single Olympic Village for the first time. It was purpose built in the Los Angeles suburb of Baldwin Hills and covered 321 acres (130 hectares). They were housed in some 550 bungalows and there was a hospital, a library, a post office and 40 kitchens serving a variety of food to cater for all tastes. The female athletes stayed in a luxury hotel, the Chapman Park Hotel, on Wilshire Boulevard, Los Angeles.

The Olympic Motto

The Olympic Motto is 'Citius, Altius, Fortius', which is Latin for 'Faster (or swifter), Higher, Stronger'. The motto was proposed in 1894 by Baron Pierre de Coubertin, the founder of the modern Olympic Games, at the meeting in Paris that established the International Olympic Committee. De Coubertin borrowed the saying from his friend Henri Didon, a Dominican priest who was an athletics fanatic. The words are believed to have been engraved on the main entrance of the stadium where the ancient Olympic Games were held. The motto was also the name of an Olympic Games history journal from 1992 until 1997, when it was renamed the *Journal of Olympic History*.

Olympic Torch visits London in 2008

The Olympic Torch went through London on its way from Mount Olympia in Greece to Beijing in China for the 2008 Games. The Torch was lit – using the rays of the sun – on 25 March 2008, arrived in London in early April, then travelled through Europe, South America and Asia, including a leg in the foothills of Mount Everest, before arriving in Beijing in July 2008. The Torch Relay always includes a visit to the city staging the Games four years hence to stir up local interest. In 2008, around 20,000 torchbearers covered approximately 137,000 kilometres (85,125 miles) on the Relay.

Music for the Games

In June 2011, the BBC announced plans to hold a weekend of live music events as part of the countdown to London 2012. The event will take place on 3 and 4 March 2012.

Fair play Brit

In the final of the women's Individual Foil at Los Angeles 1984, British fencer Helen Seymour Guinness ended her gold-medal hopes when she informed officials that they had not scored two touches against her by her Austrian opponent Ellen Preis.

Space Games

The 1964 Games in Tokyo were telecast to the USA using Syncom 3, the first-ever geostationary communication satellite, and it was the first television programme to be beamed across the Pacific Ocean.

Seven golds for Andrianov

The USSR's Nikolai Andrianov won four gold medals in men's Gymnastics at the 1976 Games in Montreal, the All-Around title, Floor, Rings and Vault. Four years earlier, at Munich 1972, he won gold in the men's Floor competition and at Moscow 1980 he won two more gold medals (in the men's Team and Vault competitions). He also won eight other medals at the Games: five silver and three bronze.

A Rowing phenonemon

The Soviet Union's Vyacheslav Nikolayevich Ivanov won the gold medal in the men's Rowing Single Sculls at Tokyo 1964, adding to the gold medals he won in the same event at Melbourne 1956 and Rome 1960. In 1962, he won the inaugural World Rowing Championships and in addition to his triple Olympic Games gold-medal haul, he won the USSR Single Scull championship in 11 consecutive years (1956–66) and the European Rowing Championships four times (1956, 1959, 1961 and 1964).

The 'Blood in the Water' match

A match between Hungary and the Soviet Union at the Melbourne 1956 is considered to be the most infamous in water polo history and is known as the 'Blood in the Water match'. The Hungarian Revolution began on 23 October 1956 but was ruthlessly crushed by the Soviet army, ending on 10 November, at a time when most of the Hungarian team were preparing to travel to Australia for the Games. Many Hungarian athletes vowed never to return home and viewed the Water Polo match as an opportunity for revenge. Germany, Hungary, Italy, Soviet Union, USA and Yugoslavia had all qualified from their groups for the final round matches. With only two games left to play for each team, Hungary led the table by one point from Yugoslavia and two from the Soviet Union. With two points awarded for a win, the Soviets knew that victory over Hungary would draw them level with the current group leaders and give them a great chance for the gold medal; Hungary knew that a draw would guarantee them at least the silver. fighting broke out in the pool during the match. With a minute to go, and Hungary leading 4–0, the game was stopped to prevent angry Hungarians in the crowd reacting to Valentin Prokopov's punch on Ervin Zador, which caused blood to pour from the Hungarian's badly split eye. Hungary then beat Yugoslavia 2–1 to claim the gold medal, while the USSR won the bronze.

Mexico City 1968

The Mexico City 1968 Games were memorable for producing a number of firsts and a host of new world records. When the Games got under way, on 12 October, the Opening Ceremony was performed by President Gustavo Diaz Ordaz in the Estadio Olímpico Universitario. The rarefied air, although unfriendly to endurance athletes, assisted many others in breaking world records. Indeed, all of the men's races at 400 metres or less, plus the men's and women's relays, the Long Jump and Triple Jump witnessed new world records. Bob Beamon's (USA) staggering leap in the men's Long Jump of 8.90m to break the existing world record by 55cm survived for 22 years. Enriqueta Basilio, a Mexican hurdler, became the first woman to light the Olympic Flame, and sex testing for women was introduced for the first time at a Games. Other firsts included the performance of Dick Fosbury in the men's High Jump, as he showed the world his famous 'Fosbury Flop' technique (which would soon become the dominant technique in the event) and the first African gold-medal winners. The men's Triple Jump saw the world record broken on five occasions, and in the men's 100m, Jim Hines became the first sprinter officially to break the 10-seconds barrier. However, the 1968 Games will always be remembered for the acts of two athletes, Tommie Smith and John Carlos, two black Americans, who, after winning the gold and bronze medals respectively in the men's 200m, bowed their heads and gave the Black Power salute during the playing of the USA national anthem as a protest against racism in their country. A total of 112 nations sent 5,516 athletes (4,735 men, 781 women) to participate in 172 events across 23 sports. The Closing Ceremony took place on 27 October 1968.

Final medals table (top ten)

Pos.	Nation	Gold	Silver	Bronze	Total
1	USA	45	28	34	107
2	USSR	29	32	30	91
3	Japan	11	7	7	25
4	Hungary	10	10	12	32
5	East Germany	9	9	7	25
6	France	7	3	5	15
7	Czechoslovakia	7	2	4	13
8	West Germany	5	11	10	26
9	Australia	5	7	5	17
10	Great Britain	5	5	3	13

1936 Olympic Torch

At the opening of the 1936 Games in Berlin, the Olympic Torch was lit by a flame that originated from the fire at the sanctuary of the ancient Olympic Games in Olympia. This was the first time in the history of the modern Games that this had occurred, and every Games since has followed this method. During the 1934 Session, the IOC agreed to the proposal made by the Secretary-General of the Berlin Games organising committee for athletes to carry the Flame in relay from Olympia to Berlin. The IOC consulted with the NOCs of the six countries the Flame would have to pass through (Greece, Bulgaria, Yugoslavia, Hungary, Austria and Czechoslovakia) and they all unanimously supported the idea and agreed that the route planned should include each capital city. The Torch itself was made from polished steel and designed by the sculptor, Lemcke. The handle of the Torch was inscribed with the words *Fackelstaffel-Lauf Olympia-Berlin* 1936 ('1936 Berlin Olympics Torch Relay') and had the five Olympic Rings and the German eagle superimposed on it; on the lower section of the Torch the Flame's route from Olympia to Berlin (a total journey of more than 3,000 kilometres) was set out.

Marathon distance established

For the 1924 Games in Paris, the distance of the Marathon was fixed at 42.195 kilometres, the same distance that had been run at London 1908. Finland's Albin Stenroos went on to take gold in the event.

IOC member claims gold

Otto Herschmann won a silver medal as a member of the Austrian team in the Team Sabre Fencing event at Stockholm 1912. At the time Herschmann was president of the Austrian Olympic Committee. He remains the only sitting National Olympic Committee president to win a medal at an Olympic Games.

Not so happy Games

The official slogan of the 1972 Olympic Games in Munich was 'the Happy Games', and the official Emblem of the Games was a blue solar logo (the 'Bright Sun'). However, the murder of 11 Israeli athletes by Arab terrorists cast one of the darkest shadows in sporting history over the Games.

First participating nations

A total of 14 different nations were represented at the 1896 Games in Athens:

Australia • Austria • Bulgaria • Chile • Denmark
France • Germany • Great Britain • Greece – host nation
Hungary • Italy • Sweden • Switzerland • USA

Belgium and Russia entered the names of competitors but later withdrew them.

Logo athlete

At the 1976 Olympic Games in Montreal, Finland's Lasse Viren retained both his men's 5000m and 10,000m titles. After winning the 10,000m he removed his track shoes and waved them in the air to the crowd on his victory lap. The IOC accused the Finn of blatant advertising, as the logo of the shoe manufacturer could be clearly seen on the soles of his shoes. However, Viren protested his innocence, claiming that he removed the shoes as he had a blister. But the IOC suspended him from taking part in the men's 5000m Final after he qualified from his heats. Viren and the Finnish team lodged an appeal and he was readmitted to the race just two hours before the starting gun was fired.

Yifter the Shifter

Miruts Yifter's talent for long-distance running was first noticed when he joined the Ethiopian Air Force. He was called up to the Ethiopian national team for Mexico City 1968, but only made his Olympic Games debut at Munich 1972, at which he won a bronze medal in the men's 10,000m. Miruts missed Montreal 1976 – Ethiopia was among the African countries that boycotted the Games – but at Moscow 1980, Yifter won gold medals in both the men's 5000m and 10,000m, emulating Lasse Viren's (Finland) double in the Munich 1972 and Montreal 1976. His ability to accelerate almost effortlessly during a race earned him the nickname 'Yifter the Shifter'. At the 1980 Games Yifter's age was the subject of much media interest and it was reported to be somewhere between 33 and 42. He was very coy on the subject and when questioned by reporters, he said: 'Men may steal my chickens; men may steal my sheep. But no man can steal my age.'

Olympic Games talk (16)

'It's at the borders of pain and suffering that the men are separated from the boys.'
Czechoslovakia's greatest long-distance runner, **Emil Zatopek** – *a man indeed*

Falling over the line

When Swiss long-distance runner Gabrielle Andersen-Scheiss staggered into the Los Angeles Coliseum at the end of the women's Marathon at the 1984 Games in Los Angeles, she was clearly suffering from heat exhaustion. The medical team on hand allowed her to continue and it took her more than five minutes to complete the final 400 metres. She eventually fell across the finish line in 37th place.

Biondi's seven-up

US swimmer Matt Biondi won seven medals at the Seoul 1988 Games. He claimed five golds, in the men's 50m Freestyle, 100m Freestyle, 4 x 100m Freestyle Relay, 4 x 200m Freestyle Relay and 4 x 100m Medley Relay, a silver in the 100m Butterfly and a bronze in the 200m Freestyle. Biondi had already won a gold medal at Los Angeles 1984 (in the men's 4 x 100m Freestyle Relay). Then, at Barcelona 1992, he added two more gold medals (in the 4 x 100m Freestyle Relay and the 4 x 100m Medley Relay) and a silver in the men's 50m Freestyle. Overall, Biondi won 11 medals – eight gold, two silver and one bronze.

Fans boo winner

Finland's Lauri Lehtinen won the gold medal in the men's 5000m at the 1932 Games in Los Angeles, but Lehtinen was lucky not to have been disqualified by the officials after he twice blocked US runner Ralph Hill as the pair raced down the final straight. When the Finn crossed the line first, the American spectators booed, but they were soon silenced when the stadium announcer, Bill Henry, uttered the words: 'Remember, please, these people are our guests.'

First Olympic boycott

The IOC invited the Soviet Union to participate at the 1948 Games in London, but they declined the invitation.

Men's 800m Fantasy Olympic Games Final

1 2 3 4 5 6 7 8

Lane No./Athlete	Country	Medals
1 Joaquim Cruz	Brazil	Gold – Los Angeles 1984, Silver – Seoul 1988
2 Steve Ovett	GB	Gold – Moscow 1980
3 Alberto Juantorena	Cuba	Gold – Montreal 1976
4 Peter Snell	New Zealand	2 Gold – Rome 1960 and Tokyo 1964
5 Mal Whitfield	USA	2 Gold – London 1948 and Helsinki 1952
6 Paul Ereng	Kenya	Gold – Seoul 1988
7 Douglas Lowe	GB	2 Gold – Paris 1924 and Amsterdam 1928
8 Mel Sheppard	USA	Gold – London 1908, Silver – Stockholm 1912

Thai gold

At Athens 2004, weightlifter Pawina Thongsuk became the first Thai woman to win a gold medal at the Games, in the 75kg class. She lifted 122.5 kilograms in the snatch and set a new Games record of 150kg in the clean and jerk for a combined score of 272.5kg.

Medals in Summer and Winter Games

East Germany's Christa Luding-Rothenburger made history at the 1988 Games in Seoul. She won the silver medal in the women's Cycling Individual Sprint event to add to the two medals she had won a few months earlier in Speed Skating (gold in the women's 1000m and silver in the women's 500m) during the 1988 Winter Games in Calgary. She is the only person ever to win medals at both the Summer and Winter Games in the same year (it can no longer be achieved) and one of only a few athletes to win medals at both the Summer and Winter Games.

Rich Games

The 1984 Olympic Games in Los Angeles were the first since Athens 1896 to be hosted without government financing, but it still managed to return a profit of US$223m. It was only the second time that the Games had made a profit, the previous occasion being at Los Angeles 1932. *Time* magazine was so impressed with the financial success of the Games that it named the organiser, Peter Ueberroth, its 'Man of the Year'.

Bathroom gold medal

Great Britain's Don Thompson won the gold medal in the men's 50km Walk at the 1960 Games in Rome. Thompson acclimatised to the Italian heat by training in his bathroom, which he sealed and kept hot with steam kettles and heaters.

Wenlock and Mandeville go on tour

On 27 April 2011, the Queen's Guard and Beefeater versions of the London 2012 mascots, Wenlock and Mandeville, visited iconic London landmarks to celebrate the royal wedding of Prince William and Catherine Middleton that was taking place two days later. They went to Big Ben, the London Eye and Tower Bridge.

Munich 1972

The 1972 Olympic Games in Munich will be remembered for two events: Mark Spitz's incredible haul of seven gold medals in the Swimming competition, setting seven world records along the way; and the murder of 11 Israeli athletes by the Black September terrorist organisation. The Games of the XX Olympiad saw Archery reintroduced to the programme of events after a 52-year absence and Handball after 36. The 1972 Games also saw the introduction of the first-ever named Olympic mascot, a dachshund called Waldi. West Germany's Liselott Linsenhoff sent the home crowd into a frenzy when she became the first female Equestrian rider to win a gold medal in an individual event (the Dressage).

The Games also saw 17-year-old Soviet gymnast Olga Korbut win three gold medals and a silver. In the women's Pentathlon, 33-year-old Mary Peters of Great Britain set a new world record on her way to becoming the new 'golden girl' of British athletics by winning the gold medal. The Opening Ceremony took place in Munich's Olympiastadion on 26 August 1972 and was conducted by President Gustave Heinemann, while the Olympic Flame was lit by Gunter Zahn (Athletics, junior 1500m champion). Heidi Schüller (Athletics) performed the Olympic Oath, and the first ever Officials' Oath was performed by Heinz Pollay (Equestrian). A total of 121 nations sent 7,134 athletes (6,075 men, 1,059 women) to participate in 195 events across 23 sports.

Final medals table (top ten)

Pos.	Nation	Gold	Silver	Bronze	Total
1	Soviet Union	50	27	22	99
2	USA	33	31	30	94
3	East Germany	20	23	23	66
4	West Germany	13	11	16	40
5	Japan	13	8	8	29
6	Australia	8	7	2	17
7	Poland	7	5	9	21
8	Hungary	6	13	16	35
9	Bulgaria	6	10	5	21
10	Italy	5	3	10	18

Hungary for success

Rudolf Bauer, Hungary's Discus thrower, was the only non-American gold medallist in field events at Paris 1900.

Olympic Games talk (17)

'An Olympic Games medal is the greatest achievement and honour that can be received by an athlete. I would swap any world title to have won gold at the Games.'
Jeff Fenech, *Australian boxer, Los Angeles 1984*

British Long Jump double

At the 1964 Games in Tokyo, Great Britain claimed the Long Jump double gold, with Lynn Davies winning the men's event and Mary Rand the women's.

Gold for Gould

Although Mark Spitz (USA) was the dominant athlete at Munich 1972, winning seven gold medals in the Swimming competition and establishing a new world record in each of the seven events he entered, the achievements of 15-year-old Australian swimmer Shane Gould did not go unnoticed. Gould picked up three gold medals in the pool, winning the women's 200m and 400m Freestyle and the women's 200m Individual Medley, setting a new world record each time. She added a silver medal in the women's 800m Freestyle and a bronze in the women's 100m Freestyle. Gould is the only swimmer, male or female, to simultaneously hold every world record in the Freestyle events from 100m to 1500m, and the first female swimmer ever to win three gold medals at the Games in new world record times. She retired from the sport, aged just 16, a few weeks after the end of the Games.

Breaking the gender barrier

At the 1928 Olympic Games in Amsterdam, Poland's Halina Konopacka won a gold medal in the women's Discus Throw, the first gold medal ever won in a women's track and field event at the Games.

King and Queen of the court

At the 1996 Games in Atlanta, American Andre Agassi won the men's Tennis Singles gold medal. In May 1999, he became first man to win the career Golden Slam (Olympic Games, Wimbledon, Australian, French and US Opens), when he took the French title. Coincidentally, Steffi Graf, whom Agassi married in 2001, was the first woman to complete the career Golden Slam, at Seoul 1988.

Fanny Blankers-Koen (1918–2004)

1 Francina Elsje (Fanny) Koen was born on 26 April 1918 in Lage Vuursche, The Netherlands.

2 Her father, a former shot putter and discus thrower, encouraged her to take up sports; she had great talent in a variety of them.

3 Koen was advised to pick athletics, because although she was a fine swimmer, she had more chance of qualifying for the Olympic Games on the track.

4 In her third race, aged 17, she set a Dutch record in the women's 800m, but it was not a distance contested at the Games at the time.

5 She qualified for the 1936 Games in Berlin and finished fifth in the women's High Jump; she also got Jesse Owens's autograph, which became a treasured possession.

6 Koen broke her first world record, 11.0 seconds in the women's 100m in 1938.

7 She hoped to run in the 1940 Games in Helsinki, which were cancelled because of the Second World War, but in 1940 she married her coach Jan Blankers.

8 She broke many world records during the War and, in 1946, six weeks after giving birth to Fanny Jr, she won two European Championships gold medals.

9 Nicknamed the 'Flying Housewife', she dominated the 1948 Games in London, winning gold medals in the women's 100m, 200m, 80m Hurdles and 4 x 200m Relay.

10 Blankers-Koen's feat of four Athletics gold medals at one Olympic Games has never been equalled by another woman athlete and has only been matched by three men.

11 She was named Athlete of the Century by the IAAF, the world track Athletics governing body, in 1999.

12 On 25 January 2004, Fanny Blankers-Koen died, aged 85, in Hoofddorp, The Netherlands.

Did you know that?

Fanny Blankers-Koen also won a total of 58 national championships and five European titles.

Master horseman

Sweden's Henri Saint Cyr won two gold medals (in the Individual and Team Dressage) at the 1952 Games and repeated the feat in 1956, when the Equestrian events were held in Stockholm.

Olympic Games talk (18)

'The Olympic Games have been with the world since 776 BC and have only been interrupted by war, especially in the modern era.'
Bill Toomey, *American decathlete, Mexico City 1968*

London's Treble

The 2012 Olympic Games, the Games of the XXX Olympiad, will take place in London from 27 July to 12 August 2012. London, the first city to host the event three times, won the right to host the Games following a bidding process that ended in Singapore on 6 July 2005. Eight other cities entered the race: Havana, Istanbul, Leipzig, Rio de Janeiro, Madrid, Moscow, New York and Paris, with the last four (with London) reaching the final stages of the bidding process.

Did you know that?

Birmingham (1992) and Manchester (1996 and 2000) both made unsuccessful bids to host the Games in recent years.

Men's marathon winner ran only nine miles

After nine miles of the men's Marathon at St Louis 1904, US runner Frederick Lorz was totally exhausted and decided he could not complete the 26 miles in temperatures in the nineties. His manager gave him a lift in his car for the next 12 miles, but the car broke down. Lorz continued on foot back to the Olympic Stadium to collect his clothes, but when he crossed the finish line race officials thought he was the winner. He played along that he was the men's Marathon champion and was ready to accept the gold medal. The assembled press even took photographs of President Roosevelt's daughter, Alice, placing a laurel wreath over Lorz's head. However, just before the medal presentation, an official reported that he had seen Lorz passing him in a car, and Lorz finally came clean and admitted that it was a joke. The American Athletics Union (AAU) did not see the funny side of Lorz's joke, however, and banned him from the sport for life, although they reinstated him and in 1905 he won the Boston Marathon later that year.

Cameroon win shootout gold

At Sydney 2000, Cameroon beat Spain 5–3 in a penalty shootout to win the gold medal in the men's Football after the final ended 2–2.

With bow and racquet

The 1908 Games in London saw Archers William and Charlotte 'Lottie' Dod become the first brother and sister medallists at an Olympic Games. Both are descendants of Sir Anthony Dod of Edge, who commanded the British Archers at the Battle of Agincourt. William won gold in the men's Double York round, while Lottie took silver in the women's Double National round. Amazingly, neither had taken up competitive archery until 1906. Lottie was better known as a tennis player, winning the Wimbledon Ladies Singles Championships five times. When she won her first Wimbledon crown, in 1887, she was only 15 years old, and remains the youngest player to win the Ladies' Singles tournament, though Martina Hingis was three days younger when she won the women's Doubles title in 1996. In addition to archery and tennis, Lottie competed in many other sports including hockey and golf. She won the 1904 British Ladies Amateur Golf Championship at Royal Troon and helped to found, and played for, the England women's national field hockey team. *The Guinness Book of Records* named Dod as the most versatile female athletes of all time, along with the USA's Babe Zaharias (athletics and golf).

First Asian individual gold

At the 1928 Games in Amsterdam, Japan's Mikio Oda, born on 30 March 1905 in Hiroshima, won the men's Triple Jump with a leap of 15.21 metres to become the first Asian to claim a gold medal at the Games in an individual event. Oda also competed in the men's Long Jump, finishing joint 11th, and in the men's High Jump (he was joint seventh). In 1931, while a student at Waseda University in Japan, he set a new men's triple jump world record of 15.58m. Oda died on 2 December 1998, aged 93, and in 2000 a panel of track and field experts voted him the Male Asian Athlete of the Century.

Four gold medals for Greg Louganis

At the 1988 Games in Seoul, US diver Greg Louganis struck his head on the springboard while attempting a reverse 2½ pike during the qualifying round for the men's 3m Springboard event. He had stitches inserted in the wound, but made the final in which he won the gold medal to retain his title – a feat he also achieved in the 10m Platform event. In 1996, Greg released a bestselling autobiography entitled *Breaking the Surface*.

The Baron claims the silver

Great Britain's Rowing Eight were coxed to silver-medal success at the Moscow 1980 Games by Colin Moynihan (the 4th Baron Moynihan). On 5 October 2005, the former MP and Minister for Sport was elected Chairman of the British Olympic Association (BOA), beating the men's 400m Hurdles gold medallist at the 1968 Games in Mexico City David Hemery by 28 votes to 15.

Budd and Decker clash

During the women's 3000m Final at Los Angeles 1984, Zola Budd (GB) and home favourite Mary Decker tangled, causing the American athlete to stumble and fall on to the infield and out of the race. The crowd went mad with fury and, even though the barefooted Budd finished out of the medal places, in seventh, the USA team filed a protest. Budd was originally disqualified from the race, but the decision was later overturned when video evidence showed that Budd had done nothing wrong.

1976 African boycott

The 1976 Games in Montreal were boycotted by African and Asian countries following the IOC's refusal to ban New Zealand from the Games. New Zealand's national rugby team (the All Blacks) had continued to play matches with South Africa, a country banned from the Olympic Games since 1964 because of its Apartheid policies. The following 28 countries boycotted the Games:

Algeria • Cameroon • Central African Republic • Chad
Congo • Egypt • Ethiopia • Gabon • Gambia • Ghana
Guyana • Iraq • Kenya • Libya • Madagascar • Malawi
Mali • Morocco • Niger • Nigeria • Sudan • Swaziland
Tanzania • Togo • Tunisia • Uganda • Upper Volta • Zambia

Boy helps rowers to gold

During the Rowing competition at the 1900 Games in Paris, the Dutch Coxed Pair was missing a coxswain. On 26 August, a French boy was chosen from the crowd and the Dutch pair rowed to the gold medal. The young boy, believed to be no more than ten years old, joined in the Dutch Rowing team's Victory Ceremony and even had his photograph taken, but his identity and his age remain a mystery to this day.

Montreal 1976

The 1976 Olympic Games were held in Montreal, Canada, and were the most expensive in history. On 17 July 1976, HRH Queen Elizabeth II (as the Head of State of Canada) officially opened the Games, and two young athletes, Stephane Prefontaine and Sandra Henderson (aged 16 and 15, respectively), lit the Olympic Flame. The Olympic Oath was performed by Pierre Saint-Jean (Weightlifting) and the Officials' Oath by Maurice Forget (Athletics). Despite the Games being the subject of a boycott by African nations, a number of outstanding individual performances stood out. The star of the Games was the 14-year-old Romanian gymnast Nadia Comaneci who caught the attention of the world when she was awarded the first perfect ten for her performance on the Uneven Bars (she recorded six more perfect scores in other disciplines). In Volleyball, the Japanese women's team won all their matches in straight sets (with only one nation reaching double figures against them in a game). Poland's Irena Szewinska won the women's 400m to bring her wonderful career to an end, having amassed seven medals (three gold, two silver and two bronze) in five different events (the women's 100m, 200m, 400m, 4 x 100m Relay and Long Jump). A total of 92 nations sent 6,084 athletes (4,824 men, 1,260 women) to participate in 198 events across 21 sports at the Games. The Closing Ceremony took place on 1 August 1976.

Final medals table (top ten)

Pos.	Nation	Gold	Silver	Bronze	Total
1	USSR	49	41	35	125
2	East Germany	40	25	25	90
3	USA	34	35	25	94
4	West Germany	10	12	17	39
5	Japan	9	6	10	25
6	Poland	7	6	13	26
7	Bulgaria	6	9	7	22
8	Cuba	6	4	3	13
9	Romania	4	9	14	27
10	Hungary	4	5	13	22

Athletes booed

During the track and field events at the 1980 Games in Moscow, some athletes complained about the crowd booing competitors from East Germany and Poland.

Smokin' Joe

The USA's Joe Frazier won the Heavy Weight Boxing gold medal at the 1964 Olympic Games in Tokyo. In 1967, Muhammad Ali (gold medallist at Light Heavy Weight at Rome 1960) was stripped of his world heavyweight boxing championship belt after he refused to enlist in the US Army, objecting to the war in Vietnam. The following year, Frazier fought Buster Mathis for the vacant title and won it with an 11th-round knockout. During his career, Frazier fought Ali three times, winning their first encounter in 1971, but losing the following two in 1974 and 1975.

Time-lag Games

The 1960 Games in Rome were broadcast live by more than 100 television channels worldwide including, with a time-lag, the USA, Canada and Japan. American television network CBS paid the IOC US$394,000 for the right to broadcast the Games.

A Rowing success

At the 1936 Games in Berlin, Great Britain's Jack Beresford set a record by winning his fifth medal at the Games. The rower had won gold medals in the Single Sculls at Paris 1924 and in the Coxless Fours at Los Angeles 1932, and silver medals in the Single Sculls at Antwerp 1920 and as part of the Coxed Eight at Amsterdam 1928. His fifth medal in the Double Sculls was also his third gold.

Turnaround Games

At the 2000 Games in Sydney, the US men's Softball team lost three games in a row before turning things around and defeating each of the teams they had lost to en route to winning the gold medal.

Late start for the men's 100m

Great Britain's Harold Abrahams won the gold medal in the men's 100m and a silver medal in the men's 4 x 100m Relay at the 1924 Games in Paris. In the men's 100m final, held at 7.00pm on 7 July, Abrahams beat the USA's Jackson Scholz into second place, with New Zealand's Arthur Porritt winning the bronze medal. In memory of the race, Abrahams and Porritt dined together at 7.00pm on 7 July every year thereafter, until Abrahams died on 14 January 1978.

Olympic Games talk (19)

'Hard work has made it easy. That is my secret. That is why I win.'
Nadia Comaneci, *Romanian gymnast who recorded the first ever perfect 'ten' scores in the history of Gymnastics competition at the Games at Montreal 1976*

Olympic Flame goes out

A few days after the Olympic Flame was lit at the Opening Ceremony of the 1976 Olympic Games in Montreal, a rainstorm extinguished it. An official relit the Flame using his cigarette lighter but, in keeping with tradition, the Games' organisers put it out again and this time relit it using a back-up Flame taken from the original ceremonial Flame at Mount Olympia in Greece. When the Olympic Flame arrived in the Panathinaiko Stadium in Athens, to start the Torch Relay ahead of the 2004 Games in Athens, a gust of wind blew out the Flame. However, Gianna Angelopoulous-Daskalaki, a member of the Athens 2004 organising committee, quickly relit it again with the back-up Flame from Olympia.

Lost Olympiads

Three Olympiads have been lost as a result of the two World Wars:

Olympiad	Host City	Year
VI	Berlin	1916
XII	Helsinki	1940
XIII	London	1944

Did you know that?

Helsinki's Olympiastadion was a purpose-built stadium for the 1940 Games. It finally played host to the Games in 1952.

Six teams, three states, one winner

Hockey first appeared at the Games at London 1908. A total of six teams entered from three states: Great Britain was represented by a team from each of the four home nations (England, Scotland, Wales and Ireland), Germany (represented by a club team) and France (with players from three clubs). England beat France 10–1 in the first round, Scotland (4–0 winners over Germany) 6–1 in the semi-final and won the gold medal by beating Ireland 8–1 in the Final. Wales (3–1 semi-final losers to Ireland) and Scotland won bronze medals.

Redgrave's sporting moment

In 2002, Steve Redgrave's achievement of winning his fifth consecutive gold medal at the Games, at Sydney 2000, was voted the greatest sporting moment in *100 Greatest Sporting Moments*, a Channel 4 television programme.

The world's strongest man

Soviet weightlifter Vasily Ivanovich Alekseyev is generally considered to be the greatest ever Super-Heavyweight. In 1970, he set his first world record and from 1970 to 1977 he remained undefeated in his class, winning every World Championship and European Championship title in those eight years. He won the gold medal at the 1972 Games in Munich and retained his championship at Montreal 1976. However, at the 1980 Games in Moscow, he set his opening weight too high and, after three unsuccessful attempts, was eliminated. He retired from weightlifting after the 1980 Games, but his legacy remains: he was the first man to lift in excess of 600 kilograms in the triple event and set 80 world records and 81 national records during his career.

Did you know that?
Alekseyev coached the Unified Team's Weightlifting squad at the 1992 Olympic Games in Barcelona; they won ten medals, five of them gold.

Sorry, no more gold

The 1912 Games in Stockholm were the last at which solid gold medals were awarded. Winners' medals now are usually gold-coated silver.

Knocked-over gold

Ireland's Robert ('Bob') Morton Newburgh Tisdall won the gold medal in the men's 400m Hurdles at the 1932 Games in Los Angeles in a new world record time of 51.7 seconds. Because of an IOC rule existing at the time, however, his record time could not be validated, as he had hit a hurdle on his way to victory. The rules for the event were subsequently changed. When Juan Antonio Samaranch became the President of the IOC in 1980 he presented Tisdall with a Waterford crystal bowl with an image of him knocking over the last hurdle engraved into the glass.

An American heroine

America found a new heroine at Atlanta 1996 and she came in the diminutive shape of 18-year-old Kerri Strug from Tucson, Arizona. The American ladies Gymnastics team were determined to break Russia's stranglehold on the Team Competition and to win the gold medal for the first time in their history. The eyes of the world were fixed on the competition, which went into its final day with the Russians holding a narrow lead. However, in front of a packed 40,000 audience inside the Georgia Dome on 23 July 1996, the US team put on a majestic display and their Russian counterparts could only sit back and watch their lead gradually slip away. In the final rotation, the American girls had already notched up enough points to claim the gold medal, but those on the floor believed that the USA team still required a single good score on the Vault to win the gold medal. Dominique Moceanu (USA) fell on both of her vaults and recorded low scores, and so it was left to Strug, who was the last to vault for the USA. However, Kerri suffered the same fate as her team-mate, falling on her first vault and, as she got back to her feet, she shook her ankle, which she had hurt in the fall. Kerri limped to the end of the runway in preparation for her second attempt. What followed will never be forgotten by those in the Dome or the millions watching live on television: it was an Olympic Games moment that will live for ever. Kerri landed her vault perfectly on one foot, raised her arms to salute the mesmerised judges and then hopped around to raise her arms once more to salute the ecstatic crowd before collapsing in agony to the mat, holding her damaged ankle. The judges awarded her a score of 9.712 and with it the gold medal for the USA. Her coach, the legendary Bela Karolyi, carried her on to the podium to join her team-mates for the Victory Ceremony, after which she was taken to hospital, where it was discovered that she had suffered two torn ligaments in her ankle. As a result of her injury, Strug had to withdraw from the Individual All-Around Competition and the Floor Competition, two events in which she reached the Finals. She became a national celebrity after the Games and was even invited to the White House to meet President Bill Clinton.

Japanese mastery

The 1964 Olympic Games gave Japan a world stage on which to display its talent for organisation. The Games were so successful that the IOC awarded Japan three awards: the Olympic Cup, the Bonacossa Trophy and the 'Diploma of Merit'.

Chilly event

Athens 1896 saw the first-ever Swimming contests at the Games, which were held in the Bay of Zea. The water temperature was a chilly 13 degrees Celsius.

The hero from Prague

Two months before the 1968 Olympic Games opened, the USSR invaded Czechoslovakia. After the invasion, Vera Caslavska, a Czech gymnast, went into hiding before going on to attend Mexico City 1968. At the Games Caslavska won four gold medals (in the Individual All-Around, Vault, Uneven Bars and – in a tie for first place – the Floor competitions) and two silvers (in the Balance Beam and Team competitions). At the 1960 Games in Rome, Caslavska won a silver medal in the Team Competition and at Tokyo 1964 she won three golds (in the Individual All-Around, Vault and Balance Beam competitions) and one silver (in the Team Competition).

Triple diving gold

When Italy's Klaus Dibiasi won his third consecutive Platform Diving gold medal at the Montreal 1976 Games, he became the first to achieve this feat in a Diving event. His gold at Mexico City 1968 had already made him the first Italian to win an Olympic Games gold medal in a Diving event, and his 1976 medal made him the first diver to be awarded medals at four Olympiads.

Rugby enters the Olympic Games

Rugby made its first appearance at the Games at Paris 1900, but only three teams entered. A French representative side defeated Moseley Wanderers from England and a German side from Frankfurt to be crowned champions. Remarkably, the Moseley team played a full game of rugby in England the day before they left for Paris by train and boat. They arrived in Paris the following morning, played the French side that afternoon and were back in England by the next morning. Consequently, the scheduled game between Moseley and Frankfurt was cancelled and both teams were awarded the silver medal. Gold medals were not awarded at the 1900 Games in Paris. The winners received silver medals and bronze medals were awarded to the runners-up.

Moscow 1980

A USA-led boycott of the 1980 Olympic Games in Moscow reduced the number of participating nations to 80, the lowest number since Melbourne 1956, when just 72 participated. The calls for a boycott, in which USA President Jimmy Carter was the principal voice, stemmed from disapproval of the Soviet invasion of Afghanistan in December 1979. In the end, 64 nations joined the USA in boycotting the Games, including West Germany, Canada, China and Japan. However, the Games went ahead as scheduled, with the Opening Ceremony taking place on 19 July 1980 in the Grand Arena of the Central Lenin Stadium (now Luzhniki), with President Leonid Brezhnev in attendance. The lighting of the Olympic Flame was performed by Sergei Belov (Basketball), the Olympic Oath was delivered by Nikolay Andrianov (Gymnastics) and the Officials' Oath by Aleksandr Medved (Wrestling). The Games witnessed some outstanding individual performances, notably those of Soviet gymnast Aleksandr Dityatin, who won a medal in all eight men's Gymnastics events to become the first athlete to win eight medals at a single Games; Cuba's Teofilo Stevenson, who won his third successive Super Heavy Weight gold medal to become the first boxer to win the same division three times; and, in Athletics, East Germany's Gerd Wessig, who became the first male high jumper to break the world record during an Olympic Games, jumping 2.36 metres (7 feet 9 inches). Amazingly, Wessig qualified for the team only two weeks before the start of the Games. A total of 5,179 athletes (4,064 men, 1,115 women) participated in 203 events across 21 sports at the Games. The Closing Ceremony took place on 3 August 1980, during which Misha the bear cub (the mascot of the 1980 Games), appeared with a tear dropping from an eye.

Final medals table (top ten)

Pos.	Nation	Gold	Silver	Bronze	Total
1	USSR	80	69	46	195
2	East Germany	47	37	42	126
3	Bulgaria	8	16	17	41
4	Cuba	8	7	5	20
5	Italy	8	3	4	15
6	Hungary	7	10	15	32
7	Romania	6	6	13	25
8	France	6	5	3	14
9	Great Britain	5	7	9	21
10	Poland	3	14	15	32

Coxless Pairs double take

Both the gold and silver medal-winning Rowing teams in the Coxless Pairs event at the 1980 Games in Moscow were identical twins. East Germany's Bernd and Jorg Landvoigt took the gold medal, while the Soviet Union's Nikolai and Yuri Pimenov claimed the silver. Great Britain's Malcolm Carmichael and Charles Wiggin finished in the bronze-medal position.

Weightlifting lightweights

The Soviet-led boycott of the 1984 Games in Los Angeles had a bigger effect on Weightlifting at the Games than on any other sport. Of the top 100 ranked lifters in the world, no fewer than 94 – including 29 of the 30 medallists from the last World Weightlifting Championships and all ten of the defending champions from Moscow 1980 (five from the USSR, two from Cuba, one from Bulgaria and one from Czechoslovakia) – were absent. The gold medals in the ten weight categories were won by China (four), Romania, West Germany (two each), Australia and Italy.

Decathlon first

Boxing, Dumbbells, Freestyle Wrestling and the Decathlon all made their Olympic Games debut at St Louis 1904. They were all approved at the 1901 IOC Session held in Paris.

A bed of roses

Michel Theato, who was described as a French gardener, won the men's Marathon at the 1900 Games in Paris in a time of 2:59:45. Theato crossed the winning line more than 40 minutes ahead of his nearest competitor, Sweden's Ernest Fast. Meanwhile, US runner Richard Grant, who finished sixth in the race, complained to officials that a cyclist had knocked him down just as he was about to pass Theato. Other competitors claimed that Theato must have taken a short-cut during the race, pointing out that if he had run the proper course he would have been mud-spattered, like they all were. Theato was certainly a dark horse in one respect. When he crossed the finishing line a military band played 'La Marseillaise', but it has since been discovered that not only was Theato born in Luxembourg but that he also maintained his Luxembourgeois citizenship throughout his life.

Women's 800m Fantasy Olympic Games Final

Lane No./Athlete	Country	Medals
1 Doina Melinte	Romania	Gold – Los Angeles 1984
2 Pamela Jelima	Kenya	Gold – Beijing 2008
3 Ellen van Langen	Netherlands	Gold – Barcelona 1992
4 Maria Mutola	Mozambique	Gold – Sydney 2000, Bronze – Atlanta 1996
5 Sigrun Wodars	East Germany	Gold – Seoul 1988
6 Ann Packer	Great Britain	Gold – Tokyo 1964
7 Tatyana Kazankina	Soviet Union	Gold – Montreal 1976
8 Kelly Holmes	Great Britain	Gold – Athens 2004, Bronze – Sydney 2000

Olympic Games stadia

Olympic Games	Stadium
1896 Athens	Panathinaiko Stadio
1900 Paris	Vélodrome de Vincennes
1904 St Louis	Francis Field
1908 London	White City Stadium
1912 Stockholm	Stockholms Olympiastadion
1920 Antwerp	Olympisch Stadion
1924 Paris	Stade Olympique de Colombes
1928 Amsterdam	Olympisch Stadion
1932 Los Angeles	Los Angeles Memorial Coliseum
1936 Berlin	Olympiastadion
1948 London	Wembley Stadium
1952 Helsinki	Olympiastadion
1956 Melbourne	Melbourne Cricket Ground
1960 Rome	Stadio Olimpico
1964 Tokyo	National Olympic Stadium
1968 Mexico City	Estadio Olímpico Universitario
1972 Munich	Olympiastadion
1976 Montreal	Le Stade Olympique
1980 Moscow	Central Lenin Stadium
1984 Los Angeles	Los Angeles Memorial Coliseum
1988 Seoul	Jamsil Olympic Stadium
1992 Barcelona	Estadi Olímpic de Montjuic
1996 Atlanta	Centennial Olympic Stadium
2000 Sydney	Stadium Australia
2004 Athens	Olympiako Stadio Athinas 'Spyros Louis'
2008 Beijing	Beijing National 'Bird's Nest' Stadium
2012 London	Olympic Stadium

All aboard

At the 1912 Games in Stockholm, the concept of an Olympic Village was still some years away. The teams stayed in small hotels or rented rooms all over Stockholm, while the USA team stayed on board the transatlantic liner in which they had arrived.

Olympic Games talk (20)

'The Olympic Games remain the most compelling search for excellence that exists in sport, and maybe in life itself.'
Dawn Fraser, *Australian swimmer, triple gold medallist*

Mark Spitz (1950 –)

1 Mark Andrew Spitz was born on 10 February 1950 in Modesto, California, USA.

2 His family moved briefly to Hawaii before returning to California and he joined the Santa Clara Swim Club, to be coached by George Haines, in 1964.

3 One of the greatest Jewish athletes ever, Spitz went to the Maccabiah Games aged 15 and won four gold medals.

4 In 1967, aged 17, he broke his first world record: 4:10.60 in the men's 400m Freestyle.

5 Spitz went to the 1968 Games in Mexico City and won two gold medals, both in relays, and a silver in the men's 100m Butterfly.

6 He went to Indiana University, where, in 1971, he was named the top amateur athlete in the USA; his team-mates nicknamed him 'Mark the Shark'.

7 At the 1972 Games in Munich, Spitz set, or helped to set, seven new world records, all in Finals, and won a then single Games record seven gold medals.

8 As a Jewish athlete, he was evacuated from the Olympic Village during the terrorist raid on the Israeli team.

9 He retired after Munich 1972, aged 22, sharing the Olympic Games record for most gold medals – nine – with Larissa Latynina and Paavo Nurmi.

10 Spitz held the men's 100m and 200m world records in both Freestyle and Butterfly.

11 The poster of him, in swimming trunks with the seven gold medals around his neck, was the biggest-selling poster in the US in the early 1970s.

12 World Swimmer of the Year in 1969, 1971 and 1972, 42-year-old Spitz tried in vain to qualify for the 1992 Games.

Did you know that?
Mark also won five Pan-American gold medals, 31 National US Amateur Athletic Union titles, and eight US National Collegiate Athletic Association Championships. He set 33 world records.

Easing the Strain

During the London 2012 Olympic Games from 27 July to 12 August more than 2,000 extra train services will run in the capital. More than 1,500 extra train services will be provided during the 2012 Paralympic Games between 29 August and 9 September.

Coffee time for the athletes

Brazil sent a total of 69 athletes to the 1932 Games in Los Angeles, but only 24 of them actually competed. As with many nations at the time, the worldwide economic depression placed a huge financial burden on Brazil and the only way the Brazilian NOC could get the team to Los Angeles was to put them on a barge along with 25 tons of coffee. The idea was to stop off at various ports en route and sell the coffee to pay for the athletes' expenses. However, they managed to sell only US$24 worth of coffee, and at the time the USA required each person entering the country to pay US$1 head tax, which meant that 45 athletes were left aboard the barge. However, the Brazilian consulate in San Francisco soon learned of the plight of the 45 athletes and sent a courier to Los Angeles with a cheque made out in Brazilian cruzeiros to the value of US$45. By the time the courier arrived, however, the Brazilian cruzeiro had devalued so much that the cheque was now only worth US$17. To make matters worse, the cheque bounced when it was presented for payment.

Coe and Ovett trump each other

Steve Ovett won the gold medal in the men's 800m (his less favoured event) at the 1980 Olympic Games in Moscow, while his Great Britain team-mate Sebastian Coe had to settle for the silver medal. In the men's 1500m Final, Coe won gold, while Ovett could manage only a bronze in what was his favoured distance.

Finnegan's gold

Great Britain's Chris Finnegan won the Middle Weight Boxing gold medal at the 1968 Games in Mexico City, defeating the USSR's Alexey Kiselev on a majority points decision in the Final. Super Heavy Weight Audley Harrison won Britain's next gold medal, at Sydney 2000.

White Lightning strikes gold

At Montreal 1976, Cuba's Alberto Juantorena, nicknamed 'White Lightning', became the first athlete to win both the men's 400m and the 800m at the same Games. He won the men's 800m gold medal in a new world record time of 1:43.50 and, three days later, claimed the men's 400m gold in a low-altitude world record of 44.26. At Munich 1972, Juantorena went out in the men's 400m semi-finals, while in the same event at Moscow 1980, he finished fourth.

Los Angeles 1984

The 1984 Olympic Games were held in Los Angeles, California. The city had played host to the Games more than half a century earlier, in 1932, but on that occasion there were no other candidates to host them. Four years after the USA led a boycott of the 1980 Games in Moscow, the Soviet Union exacted revenge by leading a boycott of the 1984 Games. Thirteen communist bloc allies of the Soviet Union stayed away, the only Warsaw Pact country to participate being Romania (winners of a national record of 53 medals). However, despite the communist snub, a record 140 nations took part. Carl Lewis (USA) was the indisputable star of the Games, winning four gold medals and thereby equalling the feat of Jesse Owens (USA) at Berlin 1936. Los Angeles 1984 also witnessed a number of firsts: Joan Benoit (USA) won the inaugural women's Marathon; Connie Carpenter-Phinney (USA) claimed the gold medal in the first women's Cycling Road Race; Sebastian Coe (GB) retained his men's 1500m title (the first athlete to do so, excluding the Intercalated Games of 1906); and Neroli Fairhall became the first paraplegic athlete to take part in a medal event when she competed in the Archery competition from her wheelchair. Rhythmic Gymnastics, Synchronised Swimming and Windsurfing also made their first appearance at an Olympic Games. On 28 July 1984, the Games were officially opened by President Ronald Reagan, and the Olympic Flame was lit by decathlete Rafer Johnson. The Olympic Oath was performed by Edwin Moses (Athletics) and the Officials' Oath by Sharon Weber (Gymnastics). A total of 6,829 athletes (5,263 men, 1,566 women) participated in 221 events across 23 sports. The Games attracted 9,190 media personnel (4,863 broadcasters and 4,327 journalists), while 28,742 volunteers helped the Games run smoothly. The Closing Ceremony took place on 12 August 1984.

Final medals table (top ten)

Pos.	Nation	Gold	Silver	Bronze	Total
1	USA	83	61	30	174
2	Romania	20	16	17	53
3	East Germany	17	19	23	59
4	P.R. of China	15	8	9	32
5	Italy	14	6	12	32
6	Canada	10	18	16	44
7	Japan	10	8	14	32
8	New Zealand	8	1	2	11
9	Yugoslavia	7	4	7	18
10	South Korea	6	6	7	19

Royal family move men's Marathon start

The official marathon distance of 26 miles 385 yards (42.195km) was established at the 1908 Games in London. Originally, the Marathon covered a distance of 26 miles, but a further 365 yards were added at the beginning of the race, so the Royal Family could obtain a good view of the start from the balcony at Windsor Castle and the athletes could complete a half-circuit of the track at the White City stadium. This distance became official from the 1924 Games in Paris onwards.

A hungry athlete

Among the more unusual entrants in the men's Marathon at St Louis 1904 was a Cuban postman named Felix Caravajal. He had raised the funds to get to the Games by running around the central square in Havana and stopping between laps to appeal for contributions to his Olympic Games fund, shouting to passers-by from a soap box. However, having finally raised the money he needed, he then proceeded to lose it en route to the Games in a craps game in New Orleans. When he arrived in the stadium, the officials had to postpone the start of the men's Marathon for several minutes while Caravajal cut the sleeves off his shirt and the legs off his pants. He did not own any training shoes, and so had to run the race in lightweight street shoes. During the race he stopped along the route to chat with bystanders and when he got hungry he stole some peaches from a race official. He then deviated from the race route to eat some green apples from a nearby orchard. However, later in the 26-mile race, he developed stomach cramps and had to drop out for a time. Eventually Felix rejoined the race and managed to finish fourth overall.

Black protest or casual behaviour?

In the men's 400m Final at Munich 1972, the USA's Vincent Matthews and Wayne Collett claimed the gold and silver medals respectively. When the two athletes, both of whom were black, stood on the podium for the Victory Ceremony they could be seen joking with each other and twirling their medals. The IOC did not take too kindly to their actions, likening them to the Black Power protest performed by black American athletes Tommie Smith and John Carlos at Mexico City 1968. Although they protested their innocence, the IOC banned them from any future Olympic Games. Following their ban, the USA had to withdraw from the men's 4 x 400m Relay race as they did not have enough runners to take part.

Olympic Games talk (21)

'The last 15 metres were very difficult.'
Eric Moussambani, 'Eric the Eel', the swimmer from Equatorial Guinea whose time in the men's 100m Freestyle at the 2000 Olympic Games in Sydney was 1:52.72 – slower than the men's 200m world record and 50 seconds slower than any other competitor in the event

The ancient Olympic Games

Some historians claim the ancient Games began in Olympia, Greece, in 776 BC and were celebrated until AD 393. However, many myths and legends are attributed to the origin of the Ancient Olympic Games. One such myth claims that Zeus initiated the Games after his defeat of the Titan Cronus. Another legend claims that Heracles, the son of Zeus, was the creator of the Ancient Games and built the Olympic stadium and surrounding buildings as a tribute to his father. Some historians attribute the Ancient Games to Pelops, the mythical King of Olympia and the eponymous hero of the Peloponnesus, claiming that the Christian Clement of Alexandria made offerings to Pelops during the Games: 'The Olympian Games are nothing else than the funeral sacrifices of Pelops.' And yet another myth tells of King Iphitos of Elis, who is said to have consulted the Pythia (the Oracle of Delphi) in an attempt to prevent a war being waged against his people by the Spartans in the ninth century BC. The story goes that King Iphitos was advised by the Prophetess to organise a series of games in honour of the gods and that his Spartan opponent decided to stop the war during these games, which were called 'Olympic', and named after the sanctuary of Olympia where they were held. The Games were held every four years and the period between two Games became known as an 'Olympiad' – a method used by the Greeks to count years.

The greatest tickets on earth

8.8 million tickets were available for the London 2012 Olympic Games • 75 per cent of tickets went on sale to the public in March 2011 • 90 per cent of tickets cost £100 or less • 66 per cent of tickets cost £50 or less • 2.5 million tickets cost £20 or less • Young people aged 16 and under benefited from the 'Pay Your Age' scheme • People aged 60-plus paid £16 for their tickets • Almost 2 million applications were received for the men's 100m final • Big screens at Live Sites across the UK will also screen the sporting action

Athletes greeted from outer space

During the Opening Ceremony at the 1980 Games in Moscow, the crew of the Salyut 6 Space Station, Leonid Popov and Valery Ryumin, sent their best wishes to the athletes via a live satellite link-up between the Station and the Central Lenin Stadium. The cosmonauts appeared on the stadium's scoreboard.

An Aboriginal Gold

Ten days after Cathy Freeman lit the Olympic Flame at the Opening Ceremony of the 2000 Games in Sydney, the Aboriginal Australian won the women's 400m Final before a home crowd at the Olympic Stadium. Freeman's win made her the first athlete ever to light the Flame and then go on to win a gold medal at the same Games.

A truncheon for a hammer

Matt McGrath, an Irish-American policeman, first competed in the men's Hammer Throw event at the 1904 Olympic Games in St Louis (he was the reigning world record holder at the time). At London 1908, he was beaten in the Hammer Throw Final by another Irish-American policeman, the defending champion John Flanagan. However, at the 1912 Games in Stockholm, McGrath finally claimed gold. He attempted to defend his Hammer title at the 1920 Games in Antwerp, but injured his knee and had to withdraw after his second throw, taking fifth place. At the 1924 Games in Paris, two decades after his Games debut and now aged 45, McGrath won the silver medal.

Too drunk to compete

The 1968 Olympic Games in Mexico City witnessed the first drug disqualification when Hans-Gunnar Liljenwall, a Swedish competitor in the men's Modern Pentathlon, tested positive for excessive alcohol.

The first lost Olympiad

The 1912 Games in Stockholm closed on 27 July with a banquet at Restaurant Hasselbacken. There Baron Pierre de Coubertin gave a hopeful speech about the future of the Games and how the IOC was very much looking forward to the next Olympiad, to be held in Berlin in 1916. However, almost exactly two years later, on 28 July 1914, the First World War began and the 1916 Games were cancelled.

Wilkie halts dominant Americans

At the 1976 Games in Montreal, the USA men's Swimming team was so dominant that they won a staggering 12 of the 13 gold medals on offer. Amazingly, they also won ten silver medals and five bronze, making a total of 27 medals from the 39 available. The only man to prevent the USA from claiming a clean sweep of the gold medals was Great Britain's David Wilkie, who won the men's 200m Breaststroke in a new world record time of 2:19.20. Wilkie also claimed a silver in the men's 100m Breaststroke.

12 great displays without a medal

During the 1980 Olympic Games in Moscow, 12 track and field athletes achieved performances that would have won gold medals at any previous Games, but they they all ended up without a medal of any colour. In addition, the men's Long Jump competition was the most consistent in Olympic Games history, with all eight men in the final exceeding the 8-metre mark, while in the women's final, for the first time ever, three athletes all leaped 7.01m (23 feet).

Forgotten sports

At the 1894 Sorbonne Congress, when Athens was chosen to host the 1896 Olympic Games (the inaugural modern Games), many different sports were scheduled. When the first edition of the official programme advertising the 1896 Games was published, Cricket and Football were included as competitions. However, neither of these came to fruition at Athens 1896. Rowing was included in the original programme, but was cancelled on the day of the competition because of strong winds and the Yachting competition did not take place either. According to the official report from the Games, the Yachting had to be cancelled because, 'we had no proper boats for this, nor did any foreign ones appear for the contest'.

Outstanding Olympic records

Going into the 2008 Games in Beijing, three women's Athletics records at the Games set at Moscow 1980 remained unbeaten: in the Shot Put, the 22.41 metres set by East German Ilona Slupianek; East Germany's 41.6 seconds in the 4 x 100m Relay and the 1:53.43 set by Soviet runner Nadezhda Olizarenko in the 800m. None of these records were close to being broken at Bejing 2008.

GB's foreign gold winner

Although in 1908 Serbia and Montenegro were not members of the International Olympic Committee, an athlete from this Balkan state did climb the podium at London 1908. Paul Radmilovic was a member of the Great Britain men's Water Polo team that claimed gold in these Games. He also won a gold medal as a member of Great Britain's men's 4 x 200m Freestyle Relay team in the Swimming competition. Nicknamed 'Pavao', he also won gold medals in the men's Water Polo at Stockholm 1912 and at Antwerp 1920.

Brothers In arms

The USA's Rafer Johnson won the men's Decathlon gold medal at the 1960 Games in Rome, with the Republic of China's Yang Chuan-Kwang claiming the silver medal and the USSR's Vasili Kuznetsov the bronze. Johnson and Yang were training partners at the University of California at Los Angeles (UCLA) and, following the final event, the two athletes embraced and leaned against each other, completely exhausted.

The master fencer

At the 1912 Games in Stockholm, 18-year-old Nedo Nadi of Italy won the men's Individual Foil Fencing gold medal. In the First World War he was decorated by the Italian government for bravery shown while fighting for his country. Nadi won five more Fencing gold medals, using three different weapons, at the 1920 Games in Antwerp, a record for Fencing gold medals at one Games. He won in the Team Foil, and then secured gold in the Individual Foil (winning 22 of his 24 matches). His third gold medal came in the Team Epee event, and he followed this by claiming gold medals in both the Individual and Team Sabre. Nedo's younger brother, Aldo, also won three gold medals in each of the Team events and collected a silver in the Individual Sabre. Nedo retired after Antwerp 1920 and moved to South America, where he taught fencing as a profession. When he returned to his homeland a few years later, his amateur status was restored and he was President of the Italian Fencing Federation from 1935 until his death in 1940. Aldo moved to the USA in the 1930s, where he, too, became a fencing coach. The brothers' father and fencing tutor, Beppe, did not approve of the epee, which he considered an 'undisciplined' weapon, so they sneaked out of the family home and practised with it elsewhere.

Seoul 1988

The 1988 Olympic Games were held in Seoul, South Korea. The city had won the right to host the Games in 1981, after seeing off a bid from Nagoya (Japan). South Korea was the second Asian nation to host the Summer Games, following Tokyo in 1964. The Democratic People's Republic of Korea (North Korea), technically still at war with South Korea, boycotted the Games when the IOC refused their demands to be co-hosts. Cuba, Ethiopia and Nicaragua supported North Korea by staying at home.

On 17 September 1988, the Games were officially opened by President Roh Tae-woo, and the Olympic Flame was lit by Chong Son-man, Kim Won-tak and Son Mi-jong (Athletics). In an emotional moment at the Opening Ceremony, the Olympic Torch was carried into the Stadium by 76-year-old Sohn Kee-chung, the winner of the men's Marathon at the 1936 Games in Berlin, who was forced to compete for Japan as Korea was occupied by the Japanese at the time. The Olympic Oath was performed by Hur Jae (Basketball) and Son Mi-na (Handball), and the Officials' Oath was taken by Lee Hak-rae (Judo). The 1988 Games was the fourth Olympiad to be held in the autumn (and, after Tokyo 1964, the second to be held in Asia), while the Opening Ceremony (the last to be held during the daytime) featured a mass demonstration of Taekwondo with hundreds of adults and children performing various moves in unison. A total of 159 nations sent 8,391 athletes (6,197 men, 2,194 women) to compete in 237 events across 25 sports at the Games; and 52 nations won medals at the Games, 31 of them taking home gold medals. A total of 27,221 volunteers helped out at Seoul 1988, and 11,331 media personnel (6,353 broadcasters and 4,978 journalists) reported the stories from the Games to the world.

Final medals table (top ten)

Pos.	Nation	Gold	Silver	Bronze	Total
1	USSR	55	31	46	132
2	East Germany	37	35	30	102
3	USA	36	31	27	94
4	South Korea	12	10	11	33
5	West Germany	11	14	15	40
6	Hungary	11	6	6	23
7	Bulgaria	10	12	13	35
8	Romania	7	11	6	24
9	France	6	4	6	16
10	Italy	6	4	4	14

One in ten

At the 1968 Games in Mexico City, Mark Spitz, the USA's winner of two gold medals, finished second in the men's 100m Butterfly Final behind his team-mate Doug Russell. It was the first time in ten races that Spitz had lost to Russell. Four years later, at Munich, 1972, Spitz entered seven events and won a further seven gold medals.

Victory by 1/100th of a second

British swimmer Adrian Moorhouse won the gold medal in the men's 100m Breaststroke at Seoul 1988 in a time of 1:02.04, just one-hundredth of a second ahead of Hungary's Karoly Guttler, with Dimitry Volkov (USSR) third in 1:02.20. Moorhouse's biggest rival, Canada's Victor Davis, could only finish fourth in a time of 1:02.20. Davis had won the gold in the men's 200m Breaststroke at Los Angeles 1984, but died in November 1989 when he was struck by a car outside a nightclub in Sainte-Anne-de-Bellevue, a suburb of Montreal. He was only 25 years old.

The right angle

US wrestler Kurt Angle won the gold medal in the men's Freestyle Wrestling Heavyweight (90–100 kilogram) division at Atlanta 1996 despite suffering a fractured neck. After the Games, Angle went on to star in Vince McMahon's World Wrestling Entertainment (WWE) and won the WWE Championship belt four times and the World Heavyweight Championship belt once. He remains the only professional wrestler to have won a gold medal at the Games.

NBC splash-out

NBC Universal paid the IOC US$793 million for the US television broadcast rights to the 2004 Games in Athens, the highest fee paid by any country.

From the pool to the office

Great Britain's Duncan Goodhew won the men's 100m Breaststroke gold medal at Moscow 1980 and added a bronze in the men's 4 x 100m Medley Relay event. He has alopecia universalis (a total lack of body hair), which some people felt gave him an advantage over his rivals in the pool, as it made him more hydrodynamic.

Olympic Games talk (22)

'When anyone tells me I can't do anything, I'm just not listening anymore.'
Florence Griffith Joyner, *United States' athlete who raced to women's 100m gold at Seoul 1988 in world-record time*

First Winter events held

The 1908 Olympic Games in London were the first to include winter events. Four Figure Skating events were contested, but they were held months apart from most of the other events.

Vietnamese delight

Taekwondo was introduced as a medal sport at the 2000 Games in Sydney, and Vietnam won its first-ever Games medal in the competition – their first Games having been at Helsinki 1952. Hieu Ngan Tran won the silver medal in the women's 49–57 kilogram category.

First all-round athlete

At Athens 1896, Germany's Carl Schumann won three events in Gymnastics (in the Vault, Horizontal Bar and the Team Parallel Bars). He also won the men's Greco-Roman Wrestling tournament and competed in three events in Athletics (Long Jump, Triple Jump and Shot Put) as well as the Weightlifting competition.

Golden punch-Up

Hungarian swimmer Zoltan Halmay won the men's 100m and 50m Freestyle events at St Louis 1904. However, after Halmay beat the home favourite, the USA's J. Scott Leary, by just one foot in the 50m, the American judge awarded the race and the gold medal to Leary. The ruling led to a fight between the two swimmers, whereupon the judges ordered a rematch. Halmay won the re-race by six-tenths of a second (28.0 to 28.6) to claim the gold medal.

Comings and goings

Tennis was played at the Olympic Games until 1924 and reinstituted in 1988. Motor Boating was an official sport at London 1908, while Polo was played at the Games in 1900, 1908, 1920, 1924 and 1936.

Inaugural Fair Play Award

The 1964 Games in Tokyo witnessed the presentation of the IOC's inaugural 'Fair Play Award'. In the Sailing regatta, the Swedish pair of Lars Gunnar Kall and Stig Lennart Kall gave up their chances of winning the gold medal in the Flying Dutchman class when they stopped to help two fellow competitors whose boat had sunk.

First Muslim gold

When Nawal El Moutawakel (Morocco) won the inaugural women's 400m Hurdles gold medal at the 1984 Games in Los Angeles, she became the first Muslim and first African female champion at the Games. She was also the first Moroccan athlete of either sex to win an Olympic Games gold medal.

How the 2012 Games were won

The figures below show the voting of the IOC judges for the 2012 Olympic Games.

City NOC	Round 1	Round 2	Round 3	Round 4
London UK	22	27	39	54
Paris France	21	25	33	50
Madrid Spain	20	32	31	–
New York USA	19	16	–	–
Moscow Russia	15	–	–	–

Victory Ceremony

At the first ten Olympic Games of the modern era, the medals were presented at the Closing Ceremony. However, at Los Angeles 1932 each Victory Ceremony took place shortly after the end of each event, a tradition that was adopted at subsequent Games and that has become a permanent feature.

The golden boys

Great Britain's men's 4 x 100m Relay team won the gold medal at the 2004 Games in Athens in a time of 38.07 seconds. The golden quartet comprised Jason Gardener, Darren Campbell, Marlon Devonish and Mark Lewis-Francis. The highly fancied USA team had to settle for the silver medal, while Nigeria claimed an unexpected, but very welcome, bronze medal.

International Olympic Committee (2011)

There are currently 111 IOC members, 25 honorary members and two honour members (Kurt Furgler of Switzerland and Henry Kissinger of the USA). Juan Antonio Samaranch is Honorary President for life.

President

Jacques Rogge .... Belgium

Vice-Presidents

Zaiqing Yu .... People's Republic of China
Mario Pescante .... Italy
Ser Miang Ng .... Singapore
Thomas Bach .... Germany

Executive Committee

Gerhard Heiberg .... Norway
Denis Oswald .... Switzerland
René Fasel .... Switzerland
Mario Vázquez Raña .... Mexico
Frank Fredericks .... Namibia
Nawal El Moutawakel .... Morocco
Richard L. Carrión .... Puerto Rico
Craig Reedie .... Great Britain
John D. Coates .... Australia
Sam Ramsamy .... South Africa

Address:
Executive Board, Château de Vidy
1007 Lausanne, Switzerland

Spitz exonerated

After receiving the gold medal in the men's 200m Freestyle Victory Ceremony at Munich 1972, Mark Spitz waved his track shoes to salute the cheering crowd. There were accusations of commercialism, led by the USSR, but Spitz was found innocent by the IOC.

Greco-Swedish sportsmanship

In the true spirit of sportsmanship, the men's Greco-Roman Wrestling Middleweight division Final at London 1908, between two Swedes, Frithiof Martensson and Mauritz Andersson, was postponed one day to allow Martensson to recover from a minor injury. Martensson eventually won the gold medal.

Men's 1500m fantasy Olympic Games Final

Lane No./Athlete	Country	Medals
1 Jim Lightbody	USA	2 Gold – St Louis 1904 and Athens 1906*
2 Paavo Nurmi	Finland	Gold – Paris 1924
3 Sebastian Coe	GB	2 Gold – Moscow 1980 and Los Angeles 1984
4 Noureddine Morceli	Algeria	Gold – Atlanta 1996
5 Peter Rono	Kenya	Gold – Seoul 1988
6 Hicham El Guerrouj	Morocco	Gold – Athens 2004
7 Kipchoge Keino	Kenya	Gold – Mexico City 1968
8 Peter Snell	New Zealand	Gold – Tokyo 1964

* Intercalated Games

Barcelona 1992

The 1992 Olympic Games in Barcelona, saw all of the IOC countries participating for the first time since Munich 1972. Even South Africa, which had been excluded from the Olympic Games family for 32 years on account of its Apartheid policy, was now invited back into the fold. These were also the first Summer Games since the reunification of East and West Germany in 1990, as well as the reunification of North and South Yemen. The Germans competed as a unified team for the first time since Rome 1960. Athletes from the Baltic states of Estonia and Latvia represented their individual nations for the first time since Berlin 1936, while Lithuania made their first appearance since Amsterdam 1928. The remaining 12 former Soviet Republics formed a Unified Team (although the medal winners were permitted to stand under the flags of their own Republics). In the former Yugoslavia, Croatia, Bosnia and Herzegovina and Slovenia all sent athletes representing these nations for the first time. Yugoslav athletes could not compete under their flag or in team events and entered under the Olympic Games banner as independent participants.

The Opening Ceremony took place on 25 July in the Lluis Companys Olympic Stadium, where the Games were officially opened by HRH King Juan Carlos I. Antonio Rebollo (Paralympic archer) lit the Olympic Flame by firing an arrow over the top of the Olympic Cauldron, igniting gas that was released from it. The Olympic Oath was performed by Luis Doreste Blanco (Sailing) and the Officials' Oath by Eugeni Asencio (Water Polo). A total of 169 nations sent 9,356 athletes (6,652 men, 2,704 women) to compete in 257 events across 28 sports. The Closing Ceremony took place on 9 August. A total of 34,548 volunteers were in attendance along with 13,082 media (7,951 broadcasters, 5,131 journalists).

Final medals table (top ten)

Pos.	Nation	Gold	Silver	Bronze	Total
1	Unified Team (ex-USSR)	45	38	29	112
2	USA	37	34	37	108
3	Germany	33	21	28	82
4	China	16	22	16	54
5	Cuba	14	6	11	31
6	Spain	13	7	2	22
7	South Korea	12	5	12	29
8	Hungary	11	12	7	30
9	France	8	5	16	29
10	Australia	7	9	11	27

2012 Emblem unveiled

On 4 June 2007, the logo for the London 2012 Olympic Games and Paralympic Games was unveiled in a star-studded ceremony in London. The logo, designed by Wolff Ollins, depicts a jagged emblem based on the date 2012. The word 'London' appears in the first digit of the 2012 date, while the five Olympic Rings are included in the second digit. The shape of the logo for the London 2012 Paralympic Games is the same, but, in the second digit, the rings are replaced by the crescents of the Paralympic Games.

Lord Coe, Chair of the London 2012 Organising Committee, said of the logo, 'This is the vision at the very heart of our brand. It will define the venues we build and the Games we hold and act as a reminder of our promise to use the Olympic spirit to inspire everyone and reach out to young people around the world. It is an invitation to take part and be involved. We will host a Games where everyone is invited to join in because they are inspired by the Games to either take part in the many sports, cultural, educational and community events leading up to 2012 or they will be inspired to achieve personal goals.'

'London 2012 will be a great sporting summer, but will also allow Britain to showcase itself to the world,' added Tony Blair, then British Prime Minister.

Spectator becomes double champion

In 1896, John Boland, an Oxford undergraduate, travelled to Athens to attend the first modern Olympic Games as a spectator. However, his friend Thrasyvoalos Manaos, Secretary of the Athens 1896 Organising Committee, entered Boland into the Tennis competition and he won both events, the men's Singles and Doubles. In the first round of the Singles, Boland defeated Friedrich Traun, a German who had earlier been eliminated from the men's 800m. In the Final Boland beat Dionysios Kasdaglis 6–2, 6–2. Boland and Traun then teamed up for the Doubles and defeated the Greek pair Kasdaglis and Demetrios Petrokokkinos in the Final, despite losing the first set.

Britain's first rowing master

During the 1912 Games in Stockholm, Ewart Horsfall won a gold medal for Great Britain in Rowing Eights. He won a silver in the same event at Antwerp 1920 and was considered Britain's greatest rower prior to Steve Redgrave's domination of the sport.

Carl Lewis (1961–)

1 Frederick Carlton 'Carl' Lewis was born on 1 July 1961 in Birmingham, Alabama, but grew up in Willingboro, New Jersey.

2 He went to the University of Houston from 1979–83 and was coached by Tom Tellez, who was his coach throughout his career.

3 Ranked in the world's top ten in the men's long jump, 100m and the 4 x 100m relay, the USA boycott of Moscow 1980 denied him the chance to compete at the Games.

4 In May 1981, he became the world's fastest sprinter at low altitude with a men's 100m time of 10.00 seconds.

5 Lewis's leap of 8.62 metres in June 1981 was the second best of all-time in the long jump.

6 At the 1984 Olympic Games in Los Angeles, he emulated Jesse Owens by winning gold medals in the men's 100m, 200m, Long Jump and 4 x 100m Relay.

7 At Seoul 1988, Lewis won gold in the men's 100m – in a world record time of 9.83 – and Long Jump, and took silver in the men's 200m.

8 In the 1991 World Championships men's long jump final, he leapt 8.91m but was beaten by Mike Powell's world record leap of 8.95m.

9 Lewis won his third and fourth Olympic Games gold medals in the men's Long Jump at Barcelona 1992 and Atlanta 1996.

10 His nine gold medals equalled the Olympic Games record then held by Paavo Nurmi, Larissa Latynina and Mark Spitz, but the haul has since been passed by Michael Phelps.

11 He was drafted to play in both the NBA and NFL despite playing neither sport at the University of Houston.

12 Lewis retired in 1997 and was named Sportsman of the Century by the IOC, World Athlete of the Century by the IAAF and Olympian of the Century by *Sports Illustrated* magazine.

Did you know that?
In 1984, Carl Lewis was selected in the tenth round of the NBA draft by the Chicago Bulls. Lewis never played a game in the NBA.

Olympic Games talk (23)

'When I passed the Chancellor he arose, waved his hand at me and I waved back at him. I think the writers showed bad taste in criticising the man of the hour in Germany.'
Jesse Owens, *four-time gold medallist at Berlin 1936*

Johnny Weissmuller — Filmography

Johnny Weissmuller, who won five Swimming gold medals at the Olympic Games in 1924 and 1928, starred in many Hollywood movies after retiring:

Glorifying the American Girl (1929) (Paramount) — Adonis
Crystal Champions (1929) (Paramount) — Himself
Tarzan the Ape Man (1932) (MGM) — Tarzan
Tarzan and His Mate (1934) (MGM — Tarzan
Tarzan Escapes (1936) (MGM) — Tarzan
Tarzan Finds a Son! (1939) (MGM) — Tarzan
Tarzan's Secret Treasure (1941) (MGM) — Tarzan
Tarzan's New York Adventure (1942) (MGM) — Tarzan
Tarzan Triumphs (1943) (RKO Pathé) — Tarzan
Tarzan's Desert Mystery (1943) (RKO Pathé) — Tarzan
Stage Door Canteen (1943) (United Artists) — Himself
Tarzan and the Amazons (1945) (RKO Pathé) — Tarzan
Swamp Fire (1946) (Paramount) — Johnny Duval
Tarzan and the Leopard Woman (1946) (RKO Pathé) — Tarzan
Tarzan and the Huntress (1947) (RKO Pathé) — Tarzan
Tarzan and the Mermaids (1948) (RKO Pathé) — Tarzan
Jungle Jim (1948) (Columbia) — Jungle Jim
The Lost Tribe (1949) (Columbia) — Jungle Jim
Mark of the Gorilla (1950) (Columbia) — Jungle Jim
Captive Girl (1950) (Columbia) — Jungle Jim
Pypmy Island (1950) (Columbia) — Jungle Jim
Fury of the Congo (1951) (Columbia) — Jungle Jim
Jungle Manhunt (1951) (Columbia) — Jungle Jim
Jungle Jim in the Forbidden Land (1952) (Columbia) — Jungle Jim
Voodoo Tiger (1952) (Columbia) — Jungle Jim
Savage Mutiny (1953) (Columbia) — Jungle Jim
Valley of Head Hunters (1953) (Columbia) — Jungle Jim
Killer Ape (1953) (Columbia) — Jungle Jim
Jungle Man-Eaters (1954) (Columbia) — Jungle Jim
Cannibal Attack (1954) (Columbia) — Himself
Jungle Moon Men (1955) (Columbia) — Himself
Devil Goddess (1955) (Columbia) — Himself
The Phynx (1970) (Warner Bros.) — Cameo
Won Ton Ton, the Dog Who Saved
  Hollywood (1976) (Paramount) — Crewman

Did you know that?
Johnny Weissmuller has a star on the Hollywood Walk of Fame.

Olympic Torch Relay

Fire had divine connotations for the ancient Greeks. It was thought to have been stolen by Prometheus from the Greek god Zeus. The Olympic Games Torch Relay was introduced by Carl Diem, the President of the Organising Committee for the 1936 Games in Berlin. His idea was part of an effort to turn the Games into a glorification of the Third Reich. However, despite its questionable origin, the Torch Relay ceremony still exists. The Olympic Torch is now lit several months before the Opening Ceremony of the Games on the site of the ancient Olympic Games in Olympia, Greece. The ceremony is performed by 11 women (in the roles of priestesses), and the Olympic Torch is lit by the sun's rays aided by the use of a parabolic mirror. Next the Olympic Flame is handed over to the officials of the Host City in a ceremony held in the Panathinaiko Stadium, Athens, which marks the beginning of the Torch Relay. The Olympic Torch is transported to the Host City of the next Games by a variety of means, including by air as well as on foot. Other unusual means of transportation have included divers, a camel, an electronic pulse and a Native American Canoe. The Olympic Torch Relay ends on the day of the Opening Ceremony in the main stadium playing host to the Games. After being ignited, the Olympic Flame continues to burn in a specially made cauldron throughout the Games and is extinguished following the Closing Ceremony.

Two silvers, no gold

At Stockholm 1912, Sweden's Anders Ahlgren fought Finland's Ivar Bohling in the Final of the wrestling Middleweight B class. The pair wrestled for nine hours without a winner emerging and the officials declared the match a tie. Neither of the two was awarded a gold medal, both receiving silver medals instead.

'The Games must go on!'

The 1972 Games in Munich were suspended for 34 hours after the murder of 11 Israeli athletes by the Black September terrorist organisation on 5 September. The day after the massacre, a Mass was held in Munich's Olympiastadion to commemorate the victims and the flags of all the competing nations were flown at half-mast. However, while many athletes returned home and others called for the Games to be cancelled, the 84-year-old outgoing IOC President, Avery Brundage, famously insisted, 'The Games must go on!'

The popular bear cub

Misha, the official mascot of the 1980 Olympic Games in Moscow, was perhaps the most successful of all the IOC's Olympic mascots. The bear cub was used extensively during the Opening and Closing Ceremonies, was made into a animated cartoon on television and appeared on a large number of merchandise products.

Anyone for Tennis?

Lawn Tennis, for men only, was in the inaugural Olympic Games at Athens 1896 and remained on the Games programme until Paris 1924. Tennis, with events for men and women, in Singles and Doubles, was a demonstration sport at Mexico City 1968 and Los Angeles 1984 and regained its full-medal status at Seoul 1988.

The Liddell memorial

In 1991, a small memorial headstone was unveiled by Edinburgh University at Eric Liddell's previously unmarked grave in the Tientsin province of North China. Paying tribute to the athlete who won the men's 400m gold medal for Great Britain at the 1924 Games in Paris, a few simple words taken from the Book of Isaiah were engraved on the memorial: 'They shall mount up with wings as eagles; they shall run and not be weary.'

Mark's charisma

At the 1988 Games in Seoul, Mark Todd, riding Charisma, retained his Eventing Individual Olympic title to become the first rider to win successive Eventing Individual titles at the Games for 60 years. He also won one silver and two bronze medals during his career as well as recording four wins at the prestigious Badminton Horse Trials and five in the Burghley Three-Day Trials. Mark also won team gold medals at the 1990 and 1998 World Championships and at the 1997 European Championships (when the competition was open to the world). Todd and fellow equestrian Andrew Nicholson are the first New Zealanders to have competed at six Olympic Games.

A classic athlete

Micheline Ostermeyer, a noted French concert pianist, won gold medals in both the women's Discus Throw and Shot Put at London 1948.

Atlanta 1996

The 1996 Olympic Games were held in Atlanta, Georgia, USA, on what was the 100th anniversary of the modern Games. On 19 July 1996, President Bill Clinton officially opened the Games in the purpose-built 85,000-seater Centennial Olympic Stadium, with the Olympic Flame lit by perhaps the best-known sportsman in the world, the legendary boxer Muhammad Ali. The Olympic Oath was taken by Teresa Edwards (Basketball) and the Officials' Oath by Hobie Billingsly (Diving). However, just eight days into the Games, a terrorist bomb exploded during a concert in the Centennial Olympic Park, killing one person, causing the death of another from a heart attack and injuring a further 110 people.

The Games did make a profit, but Atlanta 1996 is best remembered for some remarkable sporting achievements. With his men's Long Jump victory, Carl Lewis (USA) became only the third person in Olympic Games history to win the same individual event four times and the fourth to win nine gold medals. On the track, Michael Johnson (USA) broke the men's 200m world record, in a time of 19.32 seconds, on his way to becoming the first athlete to win both the men's 200m and 400m gold medals at the same Games. In Weightlifting, Turkey's Naim Suleymanoglu became the first weightlifter to win three gold medals at the Games. All 179 NOCs sent athletes to the Games, with a total of 10,318 (6,806 men, 3,512 women) participating in 271 events across 26 sports. A record-breaking 79 nations won medals, with 53 claiming at least one gold.

At the Closing Ceremony, on 4 August, the media picked up on IOC President Juan Antonio Samaranch's speech in which he said, 'Well done Atlanta', rather than calling the Games the best yet, which he had done at every previous Closing Ceremony during his presidency.

Final medals table (top ten)

Pos.	Nation	Gold	Silver	Bronze	Total
1	USA	44	32	25	101
2	Russian Federation	26	21	16	63
3	Germany	20	18	27	65
4	China	16	22	12	50
5	France	15	7	15	37
6	Italy	13	10	12	35
7	Australia	9	9	23	41
8	Cuba	9	8	8	25
9	Ukraine	9	2	12	23
10	South Korea	7	15	5	27

The Olympic Games Creed

'The most important thing in the Olympic Games is not to win but to take part, just as the most important thing in life is not the triumph but the struggle. The essential thing is not to have conquered but to have fought well.' These words were first uttered by Ethelbert Talbote, Bishop of Central Pennsylvania, during a guest service for Olympic champions in St Paul's Cathedral. Pierre de Coubertin heard the Bishop's words, and adopted them for the Olympic Games Creed.

The first Olympic Flame

Fire did not appear at the modern Olympics until the 1928 Games in Amsterdam. Jan Wils, the man who designed Amsterdam's Olympic Stadium, included a tower (the Marathon Tower) in his design with the idea that a flame would burn throughout the duration of the Games. On 28 July 1928, an employee of the Amsterdam electricity board lit the first Olympic Flame.

Scandinavian pulling power

At Paris 1900, a team of three Danes and three Swedes beat France to win gold in the Tug of War. Only two teams competed.

Mary Lou's gold

At Los Angeles 1984, the USA's Mary Lou Retton became the first gymnast from outside Eastern Europe to win the women's Gymnastics All-Around Competition. However, because of the Soviet Union-led boycott, only one of the 11 women who won gold medals at the 1983 World Gymnastics Championships in Budapest competed in LA (Romania's Ecaterina Szabo). In Budapest, Szabo won the gold medal in the floor competition, but at Los Angeles 1984 she won golds in the Team Competition, the Balance Beam (shared with compatriot Simona Pauca), the Floor Competition and the Vault.

From right to left to gold

Karoly Takacs was a member of Hungary's world champion Pistol Shooting team but, in 1938, a grenade shattered his right hand. Takacs, who had been a right-handed pistol shooter, taught himself to shoot with his left hand and at London 1948, he won the gold medal in the Rapid-fire Pistol event.

Olympic Games talk (24)

'I hope I will be partly excused by the fact that I was simply an Indian schoolboy and did not know all about such things. In fact, I did not know that I was doing wrong, because I was doing what I knew several other college men had done, except that they did not use their own names.'

*Extract from **Jim Thorpe**'s letter to the AAU in 1913 explaining his 'professional' status as a baseball player – he was still stripped of gold medals he had won at Stockholm 1912*

No gold for the hosts

At the 1976 Olympic Games in Montreal, Canada managed to win only five silver and six bronze medals. It remains the only time that the host nation has failed to claim a single gold medal at a Games.

Olympic Games events or championships?

The term 'Olympic Games' was replaced by 'Concours Internationaux d'exercises physiques et de sport' in the official report of the sporting events of the 1900 World's Fair, which was held in conjunction with the 1900 Olympic Games in Paris. Meanwhile, at the same Games, many of the press in attendance reported competitions variously as 'International Championships', 'International Games', 'Paris Championships', 'World Championships' and 'Grand Prix of the Paris Exposition'. Baron Pierre de Coubertin is reported to have said, in an interview after the Games: 'It's a miracle that the Olympic Movement survived that celebration.'

The 1900 Games medal

The front of medals at Paris 1900 show a winged goddess with her arms raised, holding laurel branches in both hands. Behind her are a view of Paris and the monuments of the Exposition Universelle. On the back, a victorious athlete is depicted standing on a podium with his arm raised, holding a laurel branch in his right hand. A stadium and the Acropolis of Athens can be seen in the background.

China win anthem gold

The Republic of China's 'Three Principles of the People' was chosen as the best national anthem at the 1936 Games in Berlin.

Birth of the Olympic Games movement

When Baron Pierre de Coubertin announced in Paris in 1892 that he intended to re-establish the Olympic Games, he was applauded, but few actually realized the enormity of the tasks that lay ahead in organising the event. The International Olympic Committee (IOC) was created on 23 June 1894; the first Olympic Games of the modern era opened in Athens on 6 April 1896; and the Olympic Movement has gone from strength to strength ever since. The Olympic Movement includes the IOC, Organising Committees of the Olympic Games (OCOGs), the National Olympic Committees (NOCs), the International Federations (IFs), the national associations, clubs and, last but certainly not least, the athletes. It is the responsibility of the Olympic Movement to pull together all those who agree to be guided by the Olympic Charter and who recognise the authority of the IOC. The overall goal of the Olympic Movement is to contribute to building a peaceful and better world by educating youth through sport practised without discrimination of any kind in a spirit of friendship, solidarity and fair play.

Football first

At the 1900 Games in Paris, Football became the first team event to be introduced to the modern Games. Great Britain, represented in Paris by Upton Park FC, beat the host nation France 4–0 in the Final.

No women allowed

Women were not allowed to compete at Athens 1896, but one woman, a protester named Stamata Revithi, ran the Marathon route the day after Greece's Spyridon Louis won the event.

Japan's Gymnastics master

At Montreal 1976, Japanese gymnast Sawao Kato won gold medals in the men's Parallel Bars and Team competitions, plus a silver in the Individual All-Around Competition. These three medals brought his tally to 12: eight gold, three silver and one bronze, which made him the most successful male gymnast in the Olympic Games and the most successful Olympian from Japan. Kato also became one of only five athletes to have won eight or more gold medals at the Games, an elite club that now contains 11 members, ten from the Summer Games and one from the Winter Games.

The Olympic Flag

In 1913, Baron Pierre de Coubertin designed a flag for the 1914 Congress of the Olympic Movement in Paris, and in particular to celebrate its 20th anniversary. De Coubertin, the French founder of the modern Games, is said to have discovered the original Olympic Games symbol of five rings engraved on an altar-stone unearthed at Delphi, but some writers on the Games refute this claim. Robert Knight Barney (in an article entitled 'This Great Symbol: the Tricks of History' published in *Olympic Review* in 1992), indicates that de Coubertin probably got the idea from the French sports federation USFSA (Union des Sociétés Françaises des Sports Athlétiques), which used an emblem consisting of two interlocking rings. For his 1913 creation, de Coubertin chose five interlocking rings and it has been claimed that he did this to celebrate the first five modern Games of the Olympiads I, II, III, IV and V. As colours for the five Rings he chose those of the flags of all the countries that were part of the International Olympic Movement at the time. In total he used six colours: white for the cloth representing 'no borders' and black, blue, green, red and yellow for the Rings. The 1914 Congress was so in awe of the flag that the design was unanimously adopted as the flag for the International Olympic Movement. The five Rings symbolise the world's five continents, although no continent is represented by any specific ring, and are intertwined on the flag, forming a trapezium with the blue, black and red rings on top and the yellow and green rings at the bottom.

Did you know that?

Although the white background was chosen to represent no borders across the five continents on the Olympic Flag, those used at Antwerp 1920 and Seoul 1988 both had a fringe of the six colours around the white field.

Famous for being last

John Stephen Akhwari came last in the men's Marathon at Mexico City 1968, but achieved stardom in his native Tanzania for completing the race despite dislocating a knee during the course of it.

Mexico's triple treble

At Mexico City 1968 the host nation won nine medals, three gold, three silver and three bronze.

The Latin Games

The 1968 Olympic Games in Mexico City were the only ones to be held in Latin America. It was also, after Tokyo 1964, only the second Games to be held outside of Europe, Australia or the USA.

Abrahams and Liddell

While Harold Abrahams won the men's 100m gold medal at Paris 1924, his team-mate Eric Liddell won gold in the men's 400m in a new world record time of 47.6 seconds. Both athletes also participated in the men's 200m, with Liddell taking the bronze medal and Abrahams finishing sixth in the final. Fifty-six years later, at Moscow 1980, Scotland's Allan Wells won the men's 100m gold medal. Following his victory, Wells was asked if he had run the race for Abrahams, the last British Olympic Games champion at 100m, to which he replied, 'No, this one was for Eric Liddell.' Liddell was, like Wells, a Scot, though he was born in Tientsin, North China, the son of Revd and Mrs James Dunlop Liddell, who were missionaries.

The White City Stadium

Work on the White City Stadium, situated near Shepherd's Bush in west London, began in 1906 as soon as London was awarded the 1908 Olympic Games – after the original hosts Rome withdrew. Built specifically to host the Games, amazingly the first all-purpose stadium was constructed in a relatively short period of time. At the time it was widely regarded as a technological marvel. It held 68,000 people and contained a running track that was 24 feet (8 yards, 7.32 metres) wide and enclosed by a 35ft (11.67yd, 10.67m) wide, 660yd (603.5m) long cycle track. In 1985, the stadium was demolished to make way for a new building, BBC White City.

The head waiter

In the men's 800m final at Munich 1972, the USA's Dave Wottle won the gold medal using an extremely unorthodox set of tactics. Wottle settled right at the back of the field for the first 600 metres and then accelerated, overtaking one runner after another. He burst into the lead in the final metres and hung on to win the gold medal by 0.03 seconds from the favourite, Yevgeny Arzhonov of the USSR. The American, who always wore a cap during his races, was nicknamed the 'Head Waiter' thanks to his unusual tactics.

Sydney 2000

The 2000 Olympic Games were held in Sydney, Australia, and were the biggest Games to date. The Opening Ceremony took place on 15 September, with the Games officially opened by Sir William Deane, Governor-General of Australia, at Stadium Australia. Cathy Freeman (Athletics) lit the Olympic Flame, the Olympic Oath was performed by Hockey player Rechelle Hawkes, and the Officials' Oath was taken by Peter Kerr (Water Polo). Every IOC member nation participated in the Games except for Afghanistan, which had been suspended by the IOC because of the ruling Taliban's prohibition of all sports participation. Korea (South Korea) and the Democratic People's Republic of Korea (North Korea) marched together under the same flag, although the athletes competed separately.

The Games witnessed a number of firsts and some outstanding individual athletic performances. For the first time tests to detect EPO and blood doping were conducted; Taekwondo and the Triathlon were new sports to the Games programme; Colombia claimed its first-ever gold medal; Vietnam won its first medal at the Games; Susanthika Jayasinghe became the first Sri Lankan female to win a medal; and the Modern Pentathlon and Weightlifting were contested by women for the first time. Individually, German kayaker Birgit Fischer became the first woman in any sport to win medals at the Games 20 years apart, while Steve Redgrave became the first rower to win gold medals at five consecutive Games. In total 199 nations (excluding East Timor, whose four athletes competed under the IOA banner) sent 10,651 athletes (6,582 men, 4,069 women) to compete in 300 events across 28 sports. In his closing address, the outgoing IOC President, Juan Antonio Samaranch, said: 'I am proud and happy to proclaim that you have presented to the world the best Olympic Games ever.'

Final medals table (top ten)

Pos.	Nation	Gold	Silver	Bronze	Total
1	USA	40	24	33	97
2	Russia	32	28	28	88
3	China	28	16	15	59
4	Australia	16	25	17	58
5	Germany	13	17	26	56
6	France	13	14	11	38
7	Italy	13	8	13	34
8	Netherlands	12	9	4	25
9	Cuba	11	11	7	29
10	Great Britain	11	10	7	28

Weightlifting hero

Turkey's Naim Suleymanoglu became the first weightlifter in the sport's history to win three consecutive gold medals at the Games when he won the 59–64 kilogram division at Atlanta 1996. Suleymanoglu is hugely popular in Turkey, as a journalist at the Games confirmed: 'When he eats at a restaurant, nobody asks him to pay the bill; if he breaks the speed limit, he does not get fined, and the police wish him a pleasant journey.'

Athletes win coins

Up until 1991, Australia minted one-cent and two-cent bronze coins, but these coins were removed from general circulation in 1992. The coins were then melted down and turned into bronze medals, which were presented at the 2000 Olympic Games in Sydney.

Keeping things in synch

Thomas Bimis and Nikolaos Siranidis won Greece's first-ever Olympic Games medal in Diving by taking the gold medal in the men's Synchronised 3m Springboard event at Athens 2004.

To compete or not to compete

At the Opening Ceremony of the 1980 Games in Moscow, 15 teams – Andorra, Australia, Belgium, Denmark, France, Great Britain, Ireland, Italy, Luxembourg, Netherlands, Portugal, Puerto Rico, San Marino, Spain and Switzerland – marched under the Olympic Flag as opposed to their national ones. As these athletes officially competed under the Olympic Flag, it was the Olympic Hymn that was played at medal ceremonies. New Zealand competed under the New Zealand Olympic and Commonwealth Games Association flag. In protest against the USSR's invasion of Afghanistan in December 1979, there was a USA-led, 64-country boycott of the 1980 Games. These 15 countries, however, left it to their athletes to decide whether to compete.

Nadia trumped by Kornelia

Although 14-year-old Romanian gymnast Nadia Comaneci was the darling of the 1976 Games in Montreal, scoring seven perfect 'tens' en route to winning three gold medals, she was outdone by East German swimmer Kornelia Ender, who won four golds.

Women's 1500m Fantasy Olympic Games Final

Lane No./Athlete	Country	Medals
1 Gabrielle Dorio	Italy	Gold – Los Angeles 1984, Silver – Moscow 1980
2 Kelly Holmes	Great Britain	Gold – Athens 2004
3 Hassiba Boulmerka	Algeria	Gold – Barcelona 1992
4 Paula Ivan	Romania	Gold – Seoul 1988
5 Lyudmila Bragina	Soviet Union	Gold – Munich 1972
6 Svetlana Masterkova	Russia	Gold – Atlanta 1996
7 Nouria Merah-Benida	Algeria	Gold – Sydney 2000
8 Tatyana Kazankina	Soviet Union	Gold – Montreal 1976 and Moscow 1980

'I have always believed that Harold Abrahams was the only European sprinter who could have run with Jesse Owens, Ralph Metcalfe and the other great sprinters from the US. He was in their class, not only because of natural gifts – his magnificent physique, his splendid racing temperament, his flair for the big occasion; but because he understood athletics, and had given more brainpower and more willpower to the subject than any other runner of his day."

Philip Noel-Baker, *captain of Team GB at Stockholm 1912 and a Nobel Prize winner, reflecting in 1948 on Abrahams's athleticism*

Orders to shoot

On 11 September 1972, a small plane was stolen at Stuttgart airport and the German authorities received information that it was another terrorist attack following on from the massacre in Munich that had occurred less than one week earlier. It was claimed that Arab terrorists were planning to drop a bomb on the Closing Ceremony that was due to take place the same day. Georg Leber, the German Defence Minister, ordered two fighter jets to shadow the aircraft and shoot it down if it approached Munich. During the mayhem, radar contact with the plane was briefly lost before another aircraft showed up on the radar system. However, this plane turned out to be a civilian passenger plane, and the stolen plane simply disappeared and was never found.

First stay-away athletes

Long before the boycotted Games in Moscow (1980) and Los Angeles (1984), tension across Europe at the time stemming from the Russo-Japanese War meant that many of the world's top international athletes did not travel across the Atlantic for the 1904 Games in St Louis.

A fit family

At Tokyo 1964, Great Britain's Ann Packer won a silver medal in the women's 400m and a gold medal in the women's 800m. Her fiancée, Robbie Brightwell, also competed in Tokyo and won a silver medal as part of Great Britain's men's 4 x 400m Relay team. The pair later married and had three sons, two of whom, David and Ian, played professional football for Manchester City.

Steve Redgrave (1962–)

1 Stephen Geoffrey (Steve) Redgrave was born in Marlow, England, on 23 March 1962.

2 In 1981, aged just 19, he won at the Henley Royal Regatta in the Double Sculls Challenge Cup.

3 At Los Angeles 1984, Redgrave, with Richard Budgett, Martin Cross and Andy Holmes, and cox Adrian Ellison, won the men's Coxed Four gold medal.

4 In 1988, he married Ann Callaway a fellow rower at Los Angeles 1984.

5 In the men's Pairs, partnering Andy Holmes, Redgrave won a second gold medal at Seoul 1988 (and bronze with Holmes and Patrick Sweeney in the Coxed Pairs).

6 In 1990 and 1991, he was part of the British Bobsleigh team.

7 Matthew Pinsent joined Redgrave in the Coxless Pairs boat at the 1992 Games in Barcelona and they won the gold medal, Redgrave's third.

8 Moments after winning gold at Atlanta 1996, again with Pinsent, Redgrave said, 'If you ever see me in a boat again, you can shoot me.'

9 In 1999, he competed in his final World Rowing Championships and won his ninth gold medal – he competed in every non-Olympic Games year between 1981 and 1999.

10 Redgrave joined the ranks of Olympic Games immortals by winning a fifth Rowing gold medal, in the Coxless Fours (with Pinsent, James Cracknell and Tim Foster) at Sydney 2000.

11 Throughout his career, he has battled ulcerative colitis and, in 1997, was diagnosed with diabetes.

12 In 2001, Her Majesty Queen Elizabeth II invested a knighthood on Sir Steve Redgrave.

Did you know that?
In April 2006, Steve Redgrave completed his third London Marathon and raised a record £1.8 million for charity.

The Heavy Weight shooter

Viggo Jensen was Denmark's first champion at the Games. He was 21 years old when he won the gold medal in the men's Heavy Weight Boxing contest on the first day (7 April) of the inaugural modern Games in Athens in 1896. Just four days later, he finished second and third in the Rifle and Pistol Shooting events respectively.

Golden gloves

The greatest Boxing team to represent the USA at an Olympic Games is the team that went to Montreal 1976. Five members won gold medals: Leo Randolph (Fly Weight), Howard Davis Jr. (Light Weight), Sugar Ray Leonard (Light Welter Weight), Michael Spinks (Middle Weight) and Leon Spinks (Light Heavy Weight). All except Davis went on to become professional world champions. The Spinks brothers, the first siblings to win Boxing gold medals at the same Games, were also the first brothers to be world heavy weight champions.

A record Olympic Games

During the 1980 Games in Moscow, 36 world records, 39 European records and 74 Olympic Games records were set. Meanwhile, more than five million people attended the various events at the Games, 1.5 million more than had attended the 1976 Games in Montreal.

Tickets for the troops

On 14 June 2011, the London 2012 Organising Committee urged members of the Army, Navy and RAF to sign up so that they would be in with a chance of receiving free tickets for the event. A total of 10,000 tickets were made available to personnel in the Armed Services through the London 2012 Ticketshare scheme.

Four-minute Medley

In Swimming's women's 4 x 100m Medley Relay at Sydney 2000, the United States became the first women's team to swim under four minutes, claiming the gold medal in a new world record time of 3:58.30. The quartet in the final were: Barbara Bedford, Megan Quann (Jendrick), Jenny Thompson and Dara Torres.

Taylan provides delight for Turkey

In the women's Weightlifting competition at Athens 2004, Turkey's Nurcan Taylan won the gold medal in the 48kg category. Amazingly, Taylan lifted a new world record of 97.5kg in the snatch, double her bodyweight, and 112.5kg in the clean and jerk on her way to the gold medal and a new world record with a combined score of 210kg. She became the first Turkish woman in any sport to win a gold medal at the Games.

Athens 2004

In 2004 the Olympic Games returned to Athens, the home of the ancient Games and the setting for the first modern Games in 1896. Athens beat competition from rival IOC bidders Buenos Aires, Cape Town, Rome and Stockholm to win the right to host the event. The 2004 Games were officially opened in the city's Olympic Stadium on 13 August 2004 by the President of the Hellenic Republic, Konstantinos Stephanopoulos. The Olympic Flame was lit by six Torchbearers: Nikos Galis (Basketball), Dimitrios Domazos (Football), Paraskevi Patoulidou (Athletics), Akakios Kachiasvilis (Weightlifting), Ioannis Melissanidis (Artistic Gymnastics) and Nikolaos Kaklamanakis (Sailing). The Olympic Oath was performed by 19-year-old Zoi Dimoschaki (Swimming) and the Officials' Oath was taken by Lazaros Voreadis (Basketball). A total of 11,099 athletes from 201 different countries, a record attendance, participated in 301 medal events across 28 different sports – one more than at Sydney 2000 – while an estimated worldwide audience of 3.9 billion people followed every move on television in the comfort of their homes.

There were a number of notable firsts: Kiribati and Timor-Leste entered their first teams; Double Trap shooter Ahmed Almaktoum won the first gold medal for the United Arab Emirates; Ilias Iliadis claimed Greece's first ever Judo gold medal; Thai weightlifter Pawina Thongsuk became the first woman from her country to win a gold medal; and women's Wrestling was included in the programme for the first time. The outstanding athlete of the Games was American swimmer Michael Phelps, who won six gold medals and equalled the single-Games record by collecting eight medals.

The Closing Ceremony took place on 29 August 2004.

Final medals table (top ten)

Pos.	Nation	Gold	Silver	Bronze	Total
1	USA	36	39	27	102
2	China	32	17	14	63
3	Russia	27	27	38	92
4	Australia	17	16	16	49
5	Japan	16	9	12	37
6	Germany	13	16	20	49
7	France	11	9	13	33
8	Italy	10	11	11	32
9	South Korea	9	12	9	30
10	Great Britain	9	9	12	30

Losers turn winners

In 1970, Montreal was awarded the right to host the 1976 Olympic Games. The Canadian city defeated rival bids from Moscow and Los Angeles, although those cities hosted the next two Games, Moscow in 1980 and Los Angeles in 1984.

Mercenary boxer

At the 1956 Games in Melbourne, Hungary's Laszlo Papp became the first boxer to win three successive gold medals in his sport. He turned professional the following year, but could not fight in Hungary because it was a communist state and, as such, professional boxing was not permitted. Papp had to travel to Vienna to train and all of his fights were staged outside Hungary. He won the European middle weight title and, in 1964, earned the chance to fight for the world middle weight title. Sadly for him, however, the Hungarian Goverment denied Papp an exit visa because they resented the fact he had fought professionally, albeit outside the country. Papp was undefeated in the ring as a professional, with 27 wins (15 by knockout) and two draws. In 2001, two years before he died, aged 77, Papp was inducted into the International Boxing Hall of Fame.

Hockey turns blue

For the first time in history the Hockey competition at London 2012 will be contested on blue pitches. The decision to move away from the standard green pitch colour will provide high levels of contrast with the white ball and lines for players, officials and spectators. The pitches will also feature pink run-off areas.

Tennis pros

As a direct result of the difficulties determining the amateur status of players, Tennis was removed from the Olympic Games programme after Paris 1924. It returned as a full-medal sport at Seoul 1988.

Summer not Winter

The proposal for a winter-sports week at Stockholm 1912, featuring Figure Skating, was rejected by the Swedish organisers because they preferred to promote the Nordic Games – a quadrennial winter sporting event – instead.

Olympic Games talk (26)

'The most important thing in the Olympic Games is not winning but taking part; the essential thing in life is not conquering but fighting well.'
Pierre de Coubertin, *the founder of the modern Olympic Games, at the 1908 Games held in London*

Mind the ducks, please

At the 1928 Olympic Games in Amsterdam, Australian rower Bobby Pearce encountered an unusual hazard midway through his Single Sculls quarter-final race against France's Victor Saurin. To his astonishment, a family of ducks lay in front of him in the water. Pearce stopped to allow the ducks to pass in front of his boat – in single file – before continuing to row. Amazingly, he proceeded to win the race, to enthusiastic applause from spectators for his actions. After winning his semi-final, Pearce beat the USA's Kenneth Myers by the huge margin of 9.8 seconds in the Final. Pearce hoped that his gold medal would gain him admission to row in the Diamond Sculls at the Henley Regatta. However, the organisers denied the young Australian because, as a carpenter, he was deemed to be a labourer and thus his occupation was not a professional one. It got even worse for Pearce at home, when he returned to Sydney, as a result of the economic depression in the country. However, Lord Dewar, the Canadian whisky manufacturer, learned of Pearce's bad luck and employed him as a salesman. This was an occupation that made him eligible for Henley so, in 1931, Pearce travelled to England and won the Henley Diamond Sculls by six lengths. Then, at the 1932 Games in Los Angeles, he retained his Single Sculls title, thus becoming the first rower to win two Single Sculls gold medals.

Jeu de paume

Jeu de paume, or Real Tennis as it is better known, was an event contested for the first and only time as a medal event at the 1908 Olympic Games in London. The competition was held at the Queen's Club in West Kensington and was won by Jay Gould II (USA) with Great Britain's Eustace Miles and Neville Lytton winning the silver and bronze medals respectively. An outdoor version of the game, called *Longue paume*, was a demonstration sport at Paris 1900 and later became an exhibition event at Paris 1924.

Royal excuse me

The 1928 Games in Amsterdam were opened by Prince Hendrik, consort of Queen Wilhelmina, who had authorised her husband to deputise for her after she refused to return from holiday. It was the first time a head of state had not attended an Opening Ceremony.

An artistic swimmer

Hungary's Alfred Hajos, a double Swimming gold medallist at the 1896 Games in Athens, won the top medal in the architectural division of the art contest at Paris 1924. Specialising in sports facilities, Hajos's architectural partner was Dezso Lauber, who had represented Hungary at Tennis at the 1908 Games in London.

First black gold-medal winner

The Franco-Haitian rugby player Constantin Henriquez de Zubiera became the first black gold medallist when the French representative side won the Rugby tournament at the 1900 Games in Paris. He also competed in the Tug of War event at the Games, winning a silver medal for France.

From the Velodrome to the boatyard

As part of an innovative Cultural Olympiad project, when the construction of the Velodrome for the 2012 Games was completed, in March 2011, any left-over wood was used to build a 30-foot sea-faring boat which was being constructed at Thornham Marina in West Sussex as part of the 'Boat Project'.

The Itch of the Golden Nit

David Walliams, Miranda Hart, Catherine Tate and Rik Mayall headed up the cast of the film *The Itch of the Golden Nit*. The project was part of the London 2012 Cultural Olympiad and was funded by Legacy Trust UK and BP and supported by the BBC.

China finally

China finally won the men's Team Gymnastics competition at Sydney 2000, having finished in the silver-medal position at the two previous Games. Ukraine claimed the silver medal and Russia the bronze.

Long wait for a long run

Long-distance races for women are relatively recent additions to the Olympic Games. Joan Benoit won the first women's Marathon at the 1984 Games in Los Angeles, Olga Bondarenko (Soviet Union) won the first women's 10,000m at Seoul 1988, and China's Wang Junxia claimed in the inaugural gold medal over 5000m at Atlanta 1996.

Changes to the Opening Ceremony

The order of teams entering the stadium in the Opening Ceremony at Beijing 2008 saw a change in the format. The first and last nations remained the same, Greece first and the hosts, China, last, but the order in between was decided by the number of brush strokes required to write the nation's name in Mandarin. Thus Australia, usually in the first ten, was third from last and Team GB was 115th.

Whoops!

Brunei did not attend the 2008 Games in Beijing after missing the deadline to register their athletes for the Opening Ceremony.

A friendly neighbour

Antwerp was the Host City of the 1920 Olympic Games, but their Dutch neighbours helped out. In what was then a unique moment in the Games' history, the 12ft Dinghy event in Sailing was held in two different countries. The competition was held in Ostend, Belgium, but the final two races in the event were held in the Netherlands. One of the race markers in the second race drifted away in a tidal current, which meant the race had to be abandoned. And as the Belgians did not have the time to re-sail the race and with both teams of Dutch origin, the Belgian Olympic Committee asked the Dutch Olympic Committee to re-sail the finals in the Netherlands.

Birthday honours

It is a great honour to carry your nation's flag at the Opening Ceremony of an Olympic Games. For world No.1 tennis player Roger Federer, carrying the Swiss flag at the 2008 Games in Beijing was even more special, because he was celebrating his 27th birthday that day.

Beijing medals

At the 2008 Olympic Games in Beijing jade was used in making the medals, the first time this had occurred in the history of the Games. The winners' medals were made of gold weighing around 6 grammes each, while the silver medal was made of pure silver.

Ride on

Great Britain's Chris Boardman won the gold medal in the men's 4000m Individual Pursuit at Barcelona 1992. A full carbon-fibre framed bike manufactured by his company, Boardman Bikes, was ridden by Nicole Cooke when she won gold at the 2008 Games in Beijing, her success coming in the women's Road Race.

Serving up a treat

For most Olympic Games competitors, the arena is usually unfamiliar. This won't be the case for the participants in the Tennis competition at London 2012, however, because they'll be playing at the All England Lawn Tennis and Croquet Club, better known as Wimbledon. The Grand Slam event finishes just three weeks before the Games start.

A tall story

The organisers of the Opening Ceremony at Beijing 2008 set a minimum height requirement of 1.70 metres (5ft 7in) for all the performers.

Innovative pricing for London 2012

Tickets for the 2012 Olympic Games in London were aimed at every pocket, but the organisers were imaginative in pricing the Opening Ceremony on Friday, 27 July 2012: the cheapest tickets are £20.12 and the most expensive are £2,012. For most sports, adults' tickets in the early rounds start at £20 for an individual session.

City before country

When choosing a location for the Summer Olympic Games, the International Olympic Committee specifically hands the honour of hosting the Games to a city rather than to a country – thus the 2012 Games will be attributed to London rather than to England.

Nadal's golden moment

When Rafael Nadal won the US Open in September 2010 he became only the second male tennis player (Andre Agassi was the first) to win a Career Golden Slam – meaning that he has won all four Grand Slams and an Olympic Games gold medal. Nadal won the Singles competition at Beijing 2008.

London Aquatics Centre

The Aquatics Centre will be the venue for Swimming (except the 10km Marathon), Diving, Synchronised Swimming and the swimming discipline of the Modern Pentathlon at London 2012, as well as for all of the Swimming events at the 2012 Paralympic Games. It is situated at the south-east corner of the Olympic Park, close to its entrance, and it is estimated that around two-thirds of spectators entering the Park will cross a giant footbridge that runs over the top of the Centre. Iraqi-born international architect Zaha Hadid is responsible for the design of the Aquatics Centre, which features a roof measuring 160 x 80 metres, giving it a longer single span than Heathrow Terminal 5. In keeping with the 2012 Games' legacy policy, after the Games, the Aquatics Centre will be transformed into a facility for the local community, clubs and schools, as well as elite swimmers.

London 2012 Marathon route

The course for the Marathon (for men and women) at London 2012 breaks with tradition as the race does not finish in the Olympic Stadium. If it was staged exclusively on the track of the Olympic Stadium, the runners would need to complete almost 105 laps of the inside lane.

When Irish eyes are smiling

At the 1956 Olympic Games in Melbourne, Ronald Michael Delany became the first Irishman to win a gold medal in Athletics at the Games since Bob Tisdall. Delany took gold in the men's 1500m in a time of 3:41.02.

Pool princess

Charlene, Princess of Monaco (neé Wittstock) represented South Africa in the 4 x 400m Medley Relay at the Sydney 2000 Games.

The Paralympic Games

The Paralympic Games can be traced back to the sports events for disabled athletes held at Stoke Mandeville in 1948, soon after the 1948 Olympic Games in London. The first official Paralympic Games were staged in Rome in 1960, although the term Paralympic only came into regular usage for the 1988 Paralaympic Games in Seoul.

Competitions in the park

At the London 2012 Games, all of the Equestrian events will take place in Greenwich Park, London's oldest royal park. It will also host the combined running and shooting event of the Modern Pentathlon.

Sprint doubles

The following men have completed the sprint double of 100m and 200m gold medals in Athletics:

Name	Country	Host City	Year
Archie Hahn	USA	St Louis	1904
Ralph Craig	USA	Stockholm	1912
Percy Williams	CAN	Amsterdam	1928
Eddie Tolan	USA	Los Angeles	1932
Jesse Owens	USA	Berlin	1936
Bobby Morrow	USA	Melbourne	1956
Valery Borzov	USSR	Munich	1972
Carl Lewis	USA	Los Angeles	1984
Usain Bolt	JAM	Beijing	2008

Did you know that?
At the 1996 Games in Atlanta, the USA's Michael Johnson won the men's 200m and 400m gold medals – the only time that the long sprint double has been achieved.

Much in demand

Fans interested in buying tickets for the 2012 Olympic and Paralympic Games in London were invited to register on a dedicated website. Registration began on 22 March 2010 and, within a matter of days, more than one million fans had registered. Around 8.8 million tickets were available for the Olympic Games and a further two million for the Paralympic Games.

Men's 10,000m fantasy Olympic Games Final

Lane No./Athlete	Country	Medals
1 Vladimir Kuts	Soviet Union	Gold – Melbourne 1956
2 Lasse Viren	Finland	Gold – Munich 1968 and Montreal 1976
3 Emil Zatopek	Czechoslovakia	Gold – London 1948 and Helsinki 1952
4 Haile Gebrselassie	Tunisia	Gold – Sydney 2000
5 Paavo Nurmi	Finland	Gold – Anwerp 1920 and Amsterdam 1928
6 Kenenisa Bekele	Ethiopia	Gold – Athens 2004 and Beijing 2008
7 Ron Clarke	Australia	Bronze – Tokyo 1964
8 Hannes Kolehmainen	Finland	Gold – Stockholm 1912

Olympic Games talk (27)

'If the Queen is watching this girl, Adlington should be made Dame. She's my best mate, so I'm allowed to say that.'
Cassie Patten, a fellow swimmer and room-mate of Great Britain's Beijing 2008 double gold medallist, Rebecca Adlington

Hooping it up

The Basketball Arena at London 2012 will be one of the few temporary stadiums. In addition to the round-robins matches in the men's and women's Basketball competition, the Arena will stage the knock-out rounds of the men's Handball, Wheelchair Basketball and Wheelchair Rugby. It is to be one of the largest-ever temporary venues built for any Games and it will be in use almost every day during the Games. The last day of Basketball at the Arena, before it transfers to the North Greenwich Arena, will be Tuesday, 7 August. The following day, the knock-out rounds of the Handball will commence. In the intervening 22 hours, the Basketball posts will be removed, the floor remarked, the Handball field of play mat laid and the Handball goals installed. Then, during the Paralympic Games, there will be just 12 hours to get ready for Wheelchair Rugby after the Wheelchair Basketball competition finishes, with similar changes needed. After the Games, the Basketball Arena will be dismantled. Parts of it are expected to be reused or relocated elsewhere in the UK.

The Queen of Dressage

At Beijing 2008, Anky van Grunsven of the Netherlands won the gold medal in the Equestrian Individual Dressage at the Hong Kong Sports Institute. Riding Salinero, she became the first rider to win the gold medal in the event three times. Her first victory, at Sydney 2000, was on Bonfire, while she partnered Salinero at Athens 2004.

Did you know that?

This was the second time that the Equestrian events had been held in a country other than that hosting the Games (Hong Kong, although a dependency of China, competes in its own right at the Olympic Games). Unlike in 1956, however, when Stockholm hosted the competition five months before the Melbourne Games, the Equestrian events were held at the same time as the Games.

Usain Bolt (1986–)

1 Usain St Leo ('Lightning') Bolt was born in Trelawny, Jamaica, on 21 August 1986.

2 A month before his 16th birthday, in July 2002, he became the youngest-ever gold medallist, winning the 200m in the World Junior Championships.

3 Bolt broke the 20-second mark for the 200m for the first time in 2004, the first junior to do so.

4 He went to the 2004 Olympic Games in Athens, but did not win a medal.

5 In 2007, Bolt broke the 32-year-old Jamaican men's 200m record, held by former Olympic Games gold medallist Don Quarrie, recording a time of 19.75 seconds.

6 In May 2008, he set a new men's 100m world record – 9.72.

7 At Beijing 2008, Bolt joined the pantheon of world sporting greats by winning gold medals in the men's 100m and 200m, both in world record times, and a gold in the men's 4 x 100m Relay.

8 Such was his domination of the men's 100m final, he actually slowed down in the final 10 metres.

9 Early in 2009, Bolt was slightly hurt in a car accident, but set a 150m street world record at the Manchester City Great Games.

10 Bolt emulated his feats at Beijing 2008 in the 2009 World Championships in Berlin, breaking his own world records to win golds in the men's 100m and 200m.

11 In recognition of his achievements, he was presented with a 12-foot-high section of the Berlin Wall. The Mayor of Berlin, in making the award, said, 'One can tear down walls that had been considered as insurmountable.'

12 A cricket lover, Usain Bolt not only bowled out the West Indies captain Chris Gayle, but when he batted, he hit a six off him too.

Did you know that?
On the blocks before the men's 100m final at Beijing 2008, Bolt was so relaxed he was laughing and waving to the crowd.

Enter the young dragon

Long Qingquan, a 17-year-old from Longshan, Hunan Province, China, won the men's Weightlifting 56 kilogram class gold medal at Beijing 2008. In his first international competition, Long was the only lifter who managed 132kg in the snatch and, in the clean and jerk, he lifted 160kg. Both lifts were also junior world records.

Lucky numbers

The number eight is considered lucky in Chinese culture so the Opening Ceremony at the 2008 Games in Beijing began at 8.08pm on Friday, 8 August 2008, or at 8.08 on 8/8/08.

North Greenwich Arena

One of the best-known landmarks in East London over the past dozen or so years will be hosting Basketball, Wheelchair Basketball, Artistic Gymnastics and Trampoline Gymnastics at the 2012 Games. The North Greenwich Arena, built on the south bank of the River Thames, opened on 1 January 2000, when it was known as the Millennium Dome, in which the Millennium Experience showcased Britain's move into the third millennium. The Dome, which cost the British tax-payer millions of pounds, closed on 31 December 2000, just as it was beginning to show signs of moving towards profitability. The venue then lay mainly vacant for a number of years – all the exhibits inside the Dome were removed – until it was bought by Anschutz Entertainment Group in 2005 and naming rights were awarded to Telefonica O_2. The venue was completely redesigned internally before reopening in 2007 and the O_2 Arena has become very popular, hosting everything from opera and rock concerts to Ultimate Fighting Championship contests and tennis tournaments. For the 2012 Games in London, the venue has been renamed the North Greenwich Arena. It is a few miles from Olympic Park, but has excellent public transport links and car parking. When the Games are over in September, the North Greenwich Arena will revert to being a multi-faceted music, sports and entertainment venue.

One and done

At the 1908 Games in London, the longest track event was the 5 miles (8,000 metres). There were six heats and a final, which was won by Emil Voigt, one of the first vegetarians to compete and medal in the Olympic Games. Voigt's time in the final was 25:11.02, a Games record that still stands, but it must be said that the five-miles race appeared only at the 1906 Intercalated Games in Athens and the 1908 Olympic Games in London. Born to German parents on 31 January 1883, in Manchester, Voigt lived in Australia for 25 years, between 1911 and 1936. He was a pioneer of early radio and set up his own radio station in Australia. Voigt died on 16 October 1973, in New Zealand.

Federer is a true champion

Swiss tennis legend Roger Federer, who has won more Grand Slam singles events than any other man, also has an Olympic Games gold medal. He partnered Stanislas Wawrinka to success in the men's Doubles at Beijing 2008, beating Sweden's Thomas Johansson and Simon Aspelin 6–3, 6–4, 6–7 (4–7), 6–3 in the final.

Outreach programme

Not all the events at London 2012 will be staged in the city and a few aren't even going to be in England. The men's and women's Football competition will have six venues: both Hampden Park, Glasgow, Scotland, and the Millennium Stadium, Cardiff, Wales, are national stadiums, as is Wembley Stadium in north-west London; and three club grounds are being used – St James' Park (home of Newcastle United FC), Old Trafford (Manchester United FC) and City of Coventry Stadium (Coventry City FC). The men's competition will comprise 16 countries and the women's 12. The first matches will be played on 25 July, two days before the Opening Ceremony. Both finals will be played at Wembley Stadium.

B team breaks world record

In the first heat of the men's 4 x 100m Freestyle Relay at Beiing 2008, the USA's Nathan Adrian, Matt Grevers, Cullen Jones and Ben Wildman-Tobriner broke the world record with a time of 3:12.23. The previous record of 3:12.46 seconds had been set in 2006, also by an American team, in Victoria, Canada. The new world record holders formed part of what was regarded as the USA's B Team. Only Jones kept his place in the team for the final, where Michael Phelps, Garret Weber-Gale, Jones and Jason Lezak proceeded to smash the world record again, clocking 3:08.24. In that final, all eight teams set new national records and the first five finished inside the world record time set a day earlier.

The Beijing 2008 Emblem

The official Emblem of the 2008 Games in Beijing was called Chinese Seal-Dancing Beijing and combined the Chinese seal and the art of calligraphy with sporting features, which transformed the image into that of a person running. The actual figure of the person resembled the Chinese character Jing, which stood for the name of the Host City.

Putting in the miles

At the 2008 Games in Beijing, Ethiopia's Kenenisa Bekele became the first man in 28 years to win gold medals in both the men's 5000m and 10,000m at the same Games. It was a triple double for Ethiopia, because not only did he retain the men's 10,000m title he had won at Athens 2004, but also his compatriot Tirunesh Dibaba became the first woman to sweep the women's 5000m and 10,000m at the same Games. They are in some elite company of long-distance legends. The other five men to have achieved the 5000m and 10,000m double at the Olympic Games were:

Athlete	Country	City	Year
Hannes Kolehmainen	Finland	Stockholm	1912
Emil Zatopek	Czechoslovakia	Helsinki	1952
Vladimir Kuts	Soviet Union	Melbourne	1956
Lasse Viren	Finland	Munich	1972
Lasse Viren	Finland	Montreal	1976
Miruts Yifter	Ethiopia	Moscow	1980

Feast fit for a king (or a small army)

Michael Phelps broke the record for most gold medals in a single Games when he won eight at Beijing 2008. The American swimmer, who also won six golds at Athens 2004, would probably win a few medals for eating, too. Standing 1.93 metres (6ft 4in) tall and weighing 85 kilograms (13st 5lb), his daily diet provided around 12,000 calories – enough for five adult men – and comprised the following:

Breakfast: Three fried egg sandwiches with cheese, tomatoes, lettuce, fried onions and mayonnaise; three chocolate-chip pancakes; a five-egg omelette; three sugar-coated slices of French toast; a bowl of grits (a maize-based porridge); two cups of coffee

Lunch: Half-kilogram (1lb) of enriched pasta; two large ham and cheese sandwiches with mayonnaise on white bread; 1,000 calories of energy drinks

Dinner: Half-kilogram of pasta, with carbonara sauce; a large pizza; 1,000 calories of energy drinks

Did you know that?

Michael Phelps was asked to describe his normal day's activities. 'Eat, sleep, swim,' he said, 'that's all I can do.'

Beijing 2008

The 2008 Olympic Games in Beijing was officially opened in the city's National Stadium (nicknamed 'The Bird's Nest') on 8 August 2008 by the President of the People's Republic of China, President Hu Jintao, before an estimated global television audience of one billion and a capacity 91,000 crowd in the stadium. More than 80 world leaders and royals, including US President George W. Bush and Russian Prime Minister Vladimir Putin, were in attendance. Beijing had won the right to host the Games by seeing off the challenges of Istanbul, Osaka, Paris and Toronto.

The Olympic Flame was lit by Li Ning, a winner of three Gymnastics gold medals at Los Angeles 1984. Li was hoisted to the roof of the stadium by wires. The Olympic Oath was performed by Zhang Yining, winner of two women's Table Tennis gold medals at Athens 2004, while the Official's Oath was taken by Huang Liping, another former Chinese gymnast.

A total of 10,708 athletes from 204 different countries (a record attendance from the National Olympic Committees), participated in 302 medal events (165 men's, 127 women's and ten mixed – one more than at Athens 2004) across 28 different sports. There were nine new events at Beijing 2008: two in the new Cycling discipline of BMX: the women's 3000m Steeplechase; and Open-water Marathon (10km) Swimming events for men and women; in addition, men's and women's Team events in Table Tennis replaced the Doubles event, while in Fencing, women's Team Foil and Team Sabre replaced the men's Team Foil and women's Team Epée. This was the last Games for both Baseball and Softball.

The Closing Ceremony took place on 24 August 2008.

Final medals table (top ten)

Pos.	Nation	Gold	Silver	Bronze	Total
1	China	51	21	28	100
2	United States	36	38	36	110
3	Russia	23	21	28	72
4	Great Britain	19	13	15	47
5	Germany	16	10	15	41
6	Australia	14	15	17	46
7	South Korea	13	10	8	31
8	Japan	9	6	10	25
9	Italy	8	9	10	27
10	France	7	16	18	41

The long and the short of it

Athletics is divided into three types of race: sprint, middle distance and long distance. The three sprint distances are 100m, 200m and 400m; middle distances are 800m, 1500m and 5000m; and long distances start at 10,000m and end with the Marathon.

Back to front

The only events at the Olympic Games in which contestants go backwards are the Rowing events, except in the Eights, when the cox is propelled forward by the oarsmen in front of him/her. Although high jumpers and pole vaulters go backwards on completing their leaps, they run forward before twisting on take-off. Kayakers, divers, and some field athletes – in the Hammer and Discus – gymnasts and Dressage riders also go backwards during their competition, but only as part of their events. Backstroke swimmers also go forwards; their stroke is so called because they swim with their backs on the water. There was one sport at the Games – discontinued after Antwerp 1920 – in which only the losers went forward: the Tug of War.

Three new faces at Beijing 2008

At the 2008 Olympic Games in Beijing, three nations participated for the first time: the Marshall Islands, Montenegro and Tuvalu. The Marshall Islands and Tuvalu are Micronesian island states in the southern Pacific Ocean, north-east and east respectively of Australia. Montenegro is a former Yugoslav Republic that gained independence from Serbia in 2006.

Eton Dorney

The Rowing venue for the London 2012 Olympic Games will hark back to London 1908 because Eton Dorney is near Windsor, from where the men's Marathon runners started their race over a century ago. As well as Rowing at Eton Dorney, there will be Canoe Sprint events and the Paralympic Rowing competitions. The venue is a 2,200-metre, eight-lane stillwater Rowing course, set in a 400-acre park with a nature conservation area. Dorney Lake is owned by Eton College and it hosted the 2005 Rowing World Cup and 2006 Rowing World Championships. A new footbridge for spectators and further temporary seating have been constructed for the London 2012 Games.

Olympic Games talk (28)

'The London Games will be designed for the athletes and we will provide them with the very best venues and the very best conditions to pursue their sporting dreams in London.'
Sebastian Coe, *Chair of the London Organising Committee for the Olympic Games (LOCOG)*

Remote control

Although the Olympic Games are awarded to a single city, the reality is that they are for the whole country. The 2012 Games in London, like those before them, will have most of the action centred in the city, but a few of the 26 Olympic sports will be staged miles away. The most remote is the Football (both the men's and women's competitions), which will have matches in Glasgow, Newcastle, Manchester, Cardiff and Coventry, as well as at Wembley. The Sailing competition will be held off the South Coast in the English Channel, close to Weymouth and Portland in Dorset. Hadleigh Farm, in Essex, is about 30 miles/45 kilometres from London and it is the venue for Cycling's Mountain Bike competition. The stillwater Rowing and Canoe events will be held 40 kilometres (25 miles) west of London at Eton Dorney, close to Windsor and Eton, while the Lee Valley White Water Centre is a few miles to the north of Stratford, at Broxbourne in Hertfordshire. Many iconic London entertainment venues will also be used: Lord's Cricket Ground (for Archery), the All England Club at Wimbledon (Tennis), Wembley Arena (Gymnastics – Rhythmic and Badminton), Hyde Park (Triathlon and Marathon Swimming), Earls Court (Volleyball), Horse Guards Parade (Beach Volleyball), The Royal Artillery Barracks (Shooting), ExCel (Boxing, Fencing, Judo, Table Tennis, Taekwondo, Weightlifting and Wrestling) and The North Greenwich Arena (Gymnastics – Artistic, Trampoline and Basketball). All the other sports will be staged at the Olympic Park and Greenwich Park areas.

Czech Republic lead medal table

For a short while, the Czech Republic led the medal table at the 2008 Games in Beijing. That's because the first gold medal of the Games was won by Katerina Emmons in the women's 10m Air Rifle Shooting event. To qualify for the final, the Czech markswoman scored a maximum 400 points, equalling the world record. She set a new Games record total of 503.5 points to win the final, with Russia's Lyubov Galinka taking silver and Croatia's Snjezana Pejcic bronze.

For your eyes only

An estimated television audience of one billion people watched the Opening Ceremony at the 2008 Olympic Games in Beijing. In the United States of America, it was shown in full, but at peak time, some 12 hours after the actual ceremony commenced, and attracted around 34.2 million viewers – the biggest television audience since the American football Super Bowl in early February. In the United Kingdom, 5.4 million watched the show live on BBC television.

Queen Anita the First

Swimmer Anita Lonsbrough, who won a gold medal in the women's 200m Breaststroke at the 1960 Olympic Games in Rome, was the first British woman to carry the flag at the Olympic Games Opening Ceremony – at the 1964 Games in Tokyo. Lonsbrough was also the first woman to win the coveted BBC Sports Personality of the Year award, in 1962, and was Great Britain's last women's Swimming gold medallist at the Olympic Games until Rebecca Adlington won two at the 2008 Games in Beijing.

Flying high

Russia's Yelena Isinbayeva broke her own women's Pole Vault world record on the way to winning her second consecutive Olympic Games gold medal at Beijing 2008. Isinbayeva beat her previous best – also the world record – by one centimetre with a clearance of 5.05 metres. It was the third time that the 26-year-old, a two-time IAAF World Championships gold medallist, had broken the world record in 2008, having earlier set new marks in Rome and Monaco.

Lightning Bolt

The most spectacular performer on the Athletics track at Beijing 2008 was Usain Bolt. The sprinter, born on 21 August 1986, in Trelawny, Jamaica, won gold medals in the men's 100m, 200m and 4 x 100m Relay and broke two world records. In the men's 100m, Bolt set a time of 9.69 seconds, a mark that would have been even better if he had not slowed down in the final 10 metres of the race. On the eve of his 22nd birthday, Bolt lined up in the men's 200m final and, despite running into a headwind, broke Michael Johnson's world record with a time 19.30. And, for good measure, he ran the third leg in Jamaica's gold medal-winning 4 x 100m Relay team.

Sebastian Coe (1956—)

1 Sebastian Coe was born in Chiswick, London, on 29 September 1956, but grew up in Sheffield, South Yorkshire.

2 In 1979, soon after leaving Loughborough University, he broke three world records in 41 days, in the men's 800m, mile and 1500m.

3 At the 1980 Games in Moscow, Coe was beaten in his preferred event, the men's 800m, by rival Steve Ovett, but turned the tables on Ovett in his favourite men's 1500m race.

4 At Los Angeles 1984, Coe again won silver in the men's 800m and gold in the men's 1500m.

5 After retiring from athletics, he moved into politics and was MP for Falmouth and Camborne between 1992 and 1997.

6 He accepted a Life Peerage to become Lord Coe in 2000 and also ran a Marathon in the time of 2:58.00.

7 Coe became an ambassador for the London 2012 bid when it was announced and joined the board of company heading the bid.

8 In 2004, when Barbara Cassani resigned, he became Chair of the London 2012 bid.

9 At the presentation of bids for the 2012 Olympic Games, Coe's presentation was particularly well received. On 6 July 2005, in Singapore, London won the right to host the 2012 Games.

10 One of the tenets of the successful bid was Lord Coe's assertion that London 2012 is not only about five weeks of summer sport, but about encouraging more people to take up sport at all levels of competition.

11 He was briefly appointed to FIFA's ethics commission, but resigned to join the committee for England to stage the FIFA Football World Cup in 2018.

12 His full title is Baron Coe of Ranmore, MBE, OBE, KBE.

Did you know that?
Sebastian Coe is a big fan of Chelsea FC.

Life will be a beach

The London 2012 Beach Volleyball competitions will be staged in the very heart of the city, on Horse Guards Parade, a short walk from Buckingham Palace and the River Thames. Horse Guards Parade, which dates from 1745, hosts the annual Trooping of the Colour celebration that takes place to mark the Queen's official birthday.

Cool runnings

Usain Bolt may have stolen the headlines at the 2008 Games in Beijing, but his Jamaican compatriots Shelly-Ann Fraser, Sherone Simpson and Kerron Stewart weren't far behind. In the women's 100m Final, the three sprinters took all of the medals, with Fraser winning in a time of 10.78 seconds. In her slipstream, nothing could separate Simpson and Stewart, so they both received silver medals. It was the first time that Jamaican athletes had taken all the places on the podium at an Olympic Games Victory Ceremony.

Britain's golden girl in the pool

When Great Britain's Rebecca Adlington won the gold medal in the women's 400m Freestyle at the 2008 Games in Beijing, with team-mate Jo Jackson taking the bronze, Adlington became the first British woman swimmer to win a gold medal for 48 years. She and Jackson were also the first to win medals of any colour since Sarah Hardcastle claimed silver in the women's 400m Freestyle and bronze in the women's 800m Freestyle at the 1984 Games in Los Angeles.

Greenwich Park

At London 2012, Greenwich Park will host the Olympic and Paralympic Equestrian competitions, as well as the riding element and the combined event of the Modern Pentathlon. Greenwich Park is London's oldest Royal Park, dating back to 1433. It has been a World Heritage Site since 1997. A temporary Cross Country course will be designed for the Park, and a temporary main arena constructed within the grounds of the National Maritime Museum. The main arena will be built on a raised platform to avoid damaging the grass.

Landmark for Kenyan women

At the 2008 Olympic Games in Beijing, Pamela Jelimo became the first Kenyan woman to win a gold medal when she won the women's 800m final. The 18-year-old set a devastating pace to win in 1:54.87 seconds, watched by 91,000 spectators inside the Bird's Nest Stadium. Janeth Jepkosgei made it a 1–2 for Kenya, by claiming the silver medal while Morocco's Hasna Benhassi completed an all-African podium with a third-place finish. Mozambique veteran Maria Mutola, the gold medallist at the 2000 Games in Sydney, who was competing at her sixth Games, finished out of the medals, in fifth place.

Index